A MOUTHFUL
OF GLASS

Lent van woerden.

A MOUTHFUL
OF GLASS

Henk van Woerden

TRANSLATED FROM THE DUTCH
BY DAN JACOBSON

Granta Books
London

Granta Publications, 2/3 Hanover Yard, London N1 8BE

First published as *Een mond vol glas* by Uitgeverij Podium 1998
First published in Great Britain by Granta Books 2000

This publication has been made possible with the financial support of the
Foundation for the Production and Translation of Dutch Literature.

A CIP catalogue record for this book is available from the British Library.

1 3 5 7 9 10 8 6 4 2

ISBN 1 86207 383 X

Typeset by M Rules

Printed and bound in Great Britain by Mackays of Chatham plc

CONTENTS

1   THE EMIGRANTS

ON 11 FEBRUARY 1955 a man could be seen wandering about the streets of Hamburg, Germany. Sometimes he halted and stared up at the branches of trees. He wore a hat but no overcoat. Absorbed in conversation with himself, he crossed Langenhorner Chaussee. It was shortly after nine in the evening; the street was empty and ill-lit. A half-hour later he entered the main gate of the General Hospital and made his way to the emergency ward.

In broken German, speaking excitedly, he told his story to the porter. He had swallowed twenty sleeping-pills, he said. Exactly twenty.

Damp snowflakes clung to his frizzy hair.

Dr Hans Nachtwey, the doctor on duty, thought the man must be either a Turk or a Syrian. He was big, with a swarthy complexion, a large nose and a double chin. His jacket was buttoned tightly across his stomach. He swayed back and forth on his chair, his arms clamped around himself. Nachtwey examined his reflexes and the pupils of his eyes. The contents of his stomach would have to be pumped out.

His father was African, his mother Greek. Or so the doctor understood him to say. This was noted down. Later in the evening Dr Nachtwey put down some other particulars about the patient. He carried a passport in the name of Demitrios Tsafendon. He was born in Lourenço Marques, the capital city of Portuguese East Africa, in 1918.

The man's agitation did not leave him. Sitting in his chair, he wept, clapped his hands to his ears, arched his back and uttered incomprehensible cries. Occasionally, without seeming to get any relief from them, he drew deep breaths into his chest. During calmer spells he let his body sink forward, as if his head had grown too heavy to hold upright. One of his hands remained on his stomach, forgotten; the other, thumb trapped inside his clenched fist, rested on the arm of the chair.

'Do you know anyone in the city?' Dr Nachtwey asked.

'I've got no problems,' the man answered hesitantly, in English.

Everything he had to say came out in fits and starts. What he would like to do, he said, was to go back to southern Africa. But it was too late now. Couldn't the doctor see how sick he was?

He opened his eyes wide: watery, amber-coloured eyes.

'It's been like this since 1937. I can't help myself. I can't defend myself. I'm always tired; always exhausted. It's eating me away.

Can't you see? And no one believes what I say. I used to have muscles, now all I've got is flabby flesh. I'm not a man any more, just half a man.'

Suddenly he burst into a screech, followed by convulsive pants and moans. There was a snake in his stomach. For years he'd carried a worm or demon inside him. Yes, he'd been examined by the doctors, many times. But they'd found nothing. It had hidden itself too deeply inside him. In the early morning he could hear it talking to him. Sometimes during the day too. He could feel it struggling in his guts.

'I'm just half a man,' he said again. 'I'll never recover now.'

'The patient is thirty-seven years old, and appears to be in good physical condition,' the doctor wrote. And beneath that, in an almost illegible hand: 'Delusional psychosis.'

Delusional. Deeply confused. The initial diagnosis was left unchanged. Tsafendon – or Tsafendas, as he also called himself – was put into the closed wing of the hospital. Enquiries made at the Hamburg Hospital for Tropical Diseases revealed that he had been examined for an infestation of tapeworm a year previously, after making similar complaints to those now heard from him. That examination had shown the parasite tormenting him to be wholly imaginary.

The man did not smoke or drink; physically his constitution was sound. Dosed with opiates and tranquillisers, he nevertheless walked in his sleep. Sometimes, standing upright, he sank into trances so deep he would lose control of his bladder and bowels; then he did not even appear to notice what had just happened to him.

At the end of the month the medication was discontinued, though no improvement in his condition had been discerned. The patient refused to get out of bed and was always ill-tempered. He barely ate. Those who tried to talk to him sooner or later heard the story of the tapeworm. Nothing would rid him of it. Also little hairy worms, he told a nurse, wriggled through his field of vision. They were like curly lines that would not disappear. Why did they never leave him alone? As for the dragon in his stomach – that had crawled into him many years before. Since then he had been its prisoner. It had taken possession of him.

'I've even drunk poison to get rid of it,' he said in confidential tones. 'Two metres of tape came out, into my underpants. But the head still remained inside. Look, they operated on me for it.' And he lifted up his pyjama jacket to show the scar of an appendix operation.

After another two weeks his condition appeared to deteriorate further. 'He urinated in the hall. He does not talk. He does not eat.' Several times the attendants had to restrain him physically. Finally it was decided to administer electric shock treatment to him.

Spring came. Hamburg thawed. With the change of season Tsafendas became calmer. Slowly but surely the storms in his head died down. He slept regularly and suddenly began to eat enough for two. His melancholy changed to a sort of nervous alertness. Even the imaginary beast in his belly retreated into the background of his consciousness. He was able to laugh, at times, with some of the hospital staff about his stupid imaginings. He winked at the nurses. He had an attractive glance under dark, caterpillar-like brows. When he felt like doing so he would tell

stories, sailors' yarns, about his experiences. Stories of wild journeys, of Alexandria, Lourenço Marques, many crossings of the
Atlantic and Indian Oceans. And about the Cape of Good Hope,
'Cabo da Bona Esperança,' as he would call it, with an unusual,
hissing emphasis. He would sing little songs the listeners could
not understand but found charming nevertheless. They liked to
hear him sing. They did not know what language he was singing
in.

One morning he stood by the window, looking out. He held his
head a little to the left, like a solemn ibis keeping watch over the
gardens of the institution. When one of the nurses found him and
asked him to come to the table for his meal, he continued to stand
there. In his best German, he asked her to pardon him for his
sickness. She responded with a reassuring pat on his plump
shoulder.

Halfway through May he was moved to another part of the
clinic, where, in expectation of their discharge, patients were
watched less closely. He offered to carry out small tasks for the
staff. And he was allowed to go for walks through the park and the
woods nearby. Now that the fever had died down, the nurses saw
him as a conversable chap, a poor seaman who had touched
bottom.

On the morning of 6 June 1955, Tsafendas bade a polite
farewell to them. He was healed, out in the streets once more. The
chestnut trees on both sides of the Langenhorner Chaussee had
already shed their flowers. He wore a faded, cinnamon-coloured
suit. A taxi took him to the centre of town.

More than eleven years later, in Cape Town, in the chamber of
the South African House of Assembly, he would kill Dr Hendrik

Verwoerd, the country's Prime Minister, with four wild stabs of the knife in his right hand.

*

6 September 1966 is inscribed sharply in my memory. At a few minutes before three in the afternoon the regular programmes of the SABC were interrupted by an urgent news item. An attack on the Prime Minister had taken place during a parliamentary sitting. It was not yet known whether or not Verwoerd had survived it.

I wandered through the botanical gardens towards the centre of the city. Outside the parliament building, at the end of a long, shady avenue, there was no sign of anything unusual going on. The spring sunshine fell indifferently on the neo-classical pediment of the building. Squirrels skipped along the gutters. I went on further, heading towards a bookshop in Long Street. Here and there groups of people stood around radios. They spoke in low tones. An hour went by. Another thirty minutes. The stillness of the town was palpable. It was true: an entire country could hold its breath. Public life had come to a halt. An unfocused anxiety seemed to rustle through the streets.

Shortly after four o'clock it was made known that the father of the nation had passed away. The architect of apartheid was dead. The Verwoerd era was over. No one dared to rejoice openly. However, many did so secretly.

In the evening I attended a small party in the upper town, above District Six. The mood in the room was one of great elation. It did not occur to anyone to doubt that the murder was the expression of a deep dissatisfaction with everything that the Afrikaners and their Nationalist Party stood for. Dissatisfaction – hatred, rather – was easy to feel. It went with being a student, in those days. Someone upstairs was keeping watch on the street below. Around the corner a black Austin had been seen with the silhouettes of two security policemen in it. A girl who had previously seemed perfectly sensible to me began to outline some instant plan of action for all of us to follow. Her voice was breaking with excitement. Her boyfriend of the moment, the journalist Gordon Winter, egged her on. (Later, much later, we were to learn that he was a police informer; eventually he chose to 'confess all' in his book *Inside BOSS: South Africa's Secret Police*.)

I retreated to the little kitchen. The hectic tone of the company roused in me a kind of loathing. Perhaps it was the lighthearted glee with which they were speaking of their 'plans' that got me down. Perhaps jealousy also had something to do with how I felt. I looked at them askance. These students had emerged from a comfortable, English-speaking milieu. They knew nothing of how life was lived in the impoverished, racially mixed suburbs in which I had grown up – on the wrong side of the tracks, as people said. They had never set foot in the Cape Flats.

In the week that followed, the assassin's motives were asserted to have been quite different from those the students had taken for granted. He was a madman; nothing else. Nothing more. In a few days Tsafendas's tapeworm had become famous nation-wide. The illusory parasite was now known to have been the invisible giver of orders: part of a plot, indeed, but a plot for which no one was to blame. Whatever political elements there may have been in

Tsafendas's statements to the police were not made known to the public. Barely any attention was given to the fact that he was of mixed parentage. The worm spoke more strongly to the imagination of the public. This suited the authorities well. Not the country but the unfortunate Greek was sick.

In October the judge presiding over the trial of Tsafendas declared that he was not fit to plead. He could not judge this man, the judge said, 'any more than I can judge a dog.' A dog? Demitrios Tsafendas was despatched to the prison on Robben Island.

The attack on Verwoerd meant as much for South Africa as the death of Kennedy had done for the United States. It was seen as a break with the past, a loss of innocence, a giant word written on the wall. But what, actually, had taken place? Was it really just a chance event, the deed of a disturbed individual, a madman?

Nothing in South Africa is simple, however, or untouched by racial awareness and racial tensions: not even madness. Or so I came to think later. And there were other aspects of the events of that day in September which were to engrave themselves on my memory. First, there was the question of colour. In general Tsafendas was spoken of simply as a Greek. But the notes taken by the doctors in Hamburg had been careless in one respect only: it was his father who had been a Cretan and his mother a black Mozambican; not, as they had said, the other way around. More striking still: Tsafendas's victim, Hendrik Verwoerd, was also the son of an emigrant.

Verwoerd was an outsider in Africa, a half-baked Hollander, just like me. The assault had been a confrontation between two immigrants. A half-Greek had murdered a half-Dutchman. The answer to many questions lay hidden in those discrepant 'halves'.

Hendrik Frensch Verwoerd was born in Amsterdam, in a house on Jacob van Lennep Quay. His mother was a Frisian, his father was from South Holland. In 1903, when Hendrik was just two years old, the family migrated to the Cape. The Anglo-Boer War had just ended. Wilhelm Verwoerd, the father, like many other Dutch people, had been much moved by the battle for their freedom fought by the Afrikaners, members of a 'brother-nation', Oom Paul Kruger's brave warriors who had been defeated and humiliated by the British. The fate of our Old Testament kins-folk who had established themselves at the foot of the African continent would continue to attract emigrants from the Netherlands for generations. The elder Verwoerd was a carpenter by trade, but his ambition was to mount the pulpit as a dominee, a clergyman of the Dutch Reformed Church. It was an ambition he never fulfilled. In the end he rose to be no more than a lay reader and a catechist. Driven into extreme poverty during the second decade of the century, Wilhelm became a hawker of Calvinistic texts and journals in the remoter districts of the Orange Free State.

His son Hendrik grew up with the High Dutch translation of the Bible, the *Statenbijbel*. He was much influenced by the anti-British sentiments of the circles in which the family moved. Until 1919, when he went to Stellenbosch University in the Cape, he spoke Dutch, not Afrikaans, at home. In the course of his parlia-mentary career his origins would become something of a sore point for him, something he preferred to play down. It was not only the opposition which grumbled that he was not a true South African; even among some of his own party, the Afrikaner Nationalists, he remained 'the Hollander'. Or worse still: the 'uitlander'. The foreigner.

Young Verwoerd was exceptionally ambitious. Ostensibly he went to Stellenbosch to study Theology and Psychology. Soon, however, he was immersed in political questions, especially those involving white poverty and the 'race question'. Appointed a university lecturer in Psychology before his twenty-third birthday, his prime concern remained the future of the 'Volk' and the developing Afrikaner Nationalist movement. At that time Afrikaners from the *platteland*, from the backveld, were being driven into the Cape peninsula in a pauperised state; inevitably they were compelled to live in the closest proximity with the Cape Coloured population. To many Afrikaners, Verwoerd among them, that could only mean national degeneration. In the early 1920s he visited the mixed suburbs of Cape Town, places like District Six and Woodstock. Scandalised by what he saw, he wrote in a university journal about this unhappy state of affairs: 'Often one finds Coloured and white families under one roof. No wonder that young Afrikaners see no objection to marrying with their former little playmates.'

Coloured or black little playmates, of course.

The migrant is an uncertain and incomplete man. He lives in an inveterate state of unease. The ultimate measure of his success is the extent to which he manages to adapt himself to the new circumstances in which he finds himself. But to what could those who are known as 'basters' – half-castes – like Demitrios Tsafendas – adapt?

Their colour was a mark they could not escape; an inheritance they could not leave behind. Why, I used to wonder as a schoolboy, were people of mixed racial origin always given names that sounded like an illness: *métique*, mulatto, half-blood, creole, bastard? To these terms was added the one always preferred by our then Prime Minister, that Dutch 'cheesehead' with a pig's nose, Verwoerd. To him they would always be Cape Coloureds. Henceforth all non-whites were condemned to live in a no-man's-land, even if it was just around the corner from us. But to those who were the product of racial mixing there clung an especial sense of shame, of scandal, a measure of self-hatred, confusion and anxiety, which Tsafendas would experience as a fault-line running right through his own body.

And Verwoerd?

His biographer says of him that he was 'the greatest gift which the Netherlands gave to South Africa in the twentieth century'. No success was denied to him in the course of his career. Academic, editor-in-chief of the Nationalist daily *Die Transvaler*, party leader, senator: always he aligned himself with well-spoken, upright, pious, respectable Afrikaners; and all this he did with an intensity that can only be explained in the light of his own back-ground. The traditional system of racial discrimination which he took over, and which, in the 1950s and subsequently, was trans-lated into the elaborate, ever more strictly enforced system of apartheid, had as its chief aim the separation of the whites of the poorer suburbs from their 'Coloured' and black fellow country-men. The aim was to establish an immovable fence between white poverty and black poverty.

One can easily see in all this the typical migrant's ambition to better himself and the condition of those like him: ex-European, ex-Dutch.

In 1950 Verwoerd was made Minister for 'Native Affairs' in the Nationalist administration. He was given unlimited power over the black population: in effect he became their dictator. No one reminded him any longer of his foreign roots, no matter how fond of pickled herring he secretly continued to be. In 1958 he became Prime Minister. Until his death eight years later he remained the Moses of the Afrikaner tribe.

Nobody questioned his leadership. Most Afrikaners felt that the gifted Verwoerd was in direct touch with both their forefathers and a transcendental realm above. He had brought his adopted people to their promised land. But did he really understand them? Enlightened members of the party complained in private that only a Hollander could have thought up his version of apartheid. His imagination was too hard in outlining policy; too inflexible and devoted to principle in putting it into effect. This immigrant's son had not 'grown up with the inheritance of his people'; or so the whisper went. He took too little account of history, or indeed of the Coloured people who, at one time, and in a half-hearted manner, had been offered the prospect of belonging to a 'brown Afrikanerdom'.

Emigration was an experience I too had undergone. My father left Leiden, in the Netherlands, for South Africa in 1956. Six months later – shortly after my ninth birthday – the rest of us followed him. The break with our country of origin was irreparable. Within a couple of years distant Holland became nothing more than a cliché. South Africa was now my home, yet it was a country in which no one appeared to feel at home.

Our local grocer was also an emigrant of a kind; he was always looked on as an outsider, a 'coolie', a 'curry-guzzler'. His fore-fathers had been shipped to the country by the Dutch East India Company. He could speak four languages and was the only person in the neighbourhood who read books, rather than strip cartoons in the newspapers. Bent over the Koran, in the half-light of his shop, he became my own image of a learned man. His shop smelt of samosas, of *bredies*, *sosaties* and other Cape Malay dishes. The faith he followed appealed in equal measure to my nostrils, my stomach and my understanding. I visited the Claremont Main Road Mosque, near a knacker's yard, about a half-hour walk from our house, and was received there in a friendly manner. I went to the Awwal Mosque in Dorp Street, on a rise above the city, where the imam repeatedly invited me to come in. Every time I did so the carpets and multi-coloured glow of light inside astonished me anew. I also made my way to the Shrine (*kramaat*) of Sheikh Yussuf of Macassar, a sacred, sweet-smelling place lost amid the windblown dunes of False Bay.

I knew next to nothing of Islam. But it seemed to me to have adapted itself in a more comely fashion to the harsh realities of southern Africa than the Dutch Reformed or Anglican churches. At the age of about twelve the faith began to exercise an irre-sistible attraction over me, both because in my eyes it was so bound up with book-learning – preserved and transmitted in a strange, attractive orthography – and because of what I perceived to be its sensuousness. The frigidly ascetic Bible classes of the Anglicans and Methodists offered nothing comparable to the recurring, resonant cries from the minaret, to the *riempie-sny*, a feast celebrated with banners and fluttering citrus leaves, and to the ceremonies of the *khalifah* or *ratiep*. My father disapproved of the last particularly: the beating drums, the dancing of those dagger-brandishing men, and then at the high point of the ritual, skewers run through cheek or lip, swords slashing at bellies, bare feet walking on burning coals – everything wonderfully without blood or blister. *Inshallah! Allahu-Akbar!*

In the early nineteen sixties the racially mixed suburb of Cape Town in which we lived was, in effect, done away with. Our Cape Coloured neighbours disappeared. I was about thirteen years old when it happened. They had gone against their will: everyone knew that. Everyone remained silent. Our scholarly grocer, who had done so much to arouse my interest in Islam, was compelled to trek along with all the others who had something 'wrong' with them. The neighbourhood bar was closed, then knocked down. I could no longer go with my sketchbook to draw the drunks who made a racket on the stoep of the bar or stretched themselves out to sleep on a patch of empty ground nearby. The mosque was left standing – it was consecrated ground – but the believers, the people whose mosque it had been, were removed from our district. It all happened very quietly. I cannot remember their departure, only a vague feeling of unease and the question: where have they gone? Not long afterwards the answer became clear. 'They' had been taken to the Cape Flats, many miles away. Our neighbourhood held its peace.

How many South Africans were chased out of their cities during those years? Three million? Four million, others say – between twelve and fifteen per cent, anyway, of the entire population of the country. And for what reason? The differences

TL CASH 1   500£ 0279 008

WATERSTONE READERS   1   12.99
            TOTAL   12.99

Cash   20.00
            Change   7.01

www.waterstones.com

between the 'poor white' Afrikaners and the Coloureds, especially, were not all that easy to make out, on either side of the colour line. Both groups spoke the same language and felt the same longing for a recognition of the wrongs done to them in the past. But what a child could not understand was this: that the war between races was always fought most fiercely when the differences between them were least apparent.

'Borderline cases,' my mother used to say. And of the awful fate that had just befallen such 'cases' she added, with a sense of shock and compassion that made a deep impression on me (and all the more so because my father did not share her sentiments): 'No wonder there's already been so many suicides and murders among them.'

Some borderline cases did their best to hide their condition. At the age of fifteen I fell in love with a classmate. Her name was Susan. She was crazy about the ballet. She had a small snub nose and bit her nails to the quick, so that the tips of her fingers swelled out above them. There was something she tried to keep secret about herself: every Sunday evening she steamed her hair and ironed it flat. Otherwise the crinkle in the hair would have become too obvious, and she would have been exposed to even more teasing than she already had to endure. I found all her characteristics attractive: her little cries, the break in her voice, the fact that she sometimes chose to read books for pleasure. Also that she gave dancing lessons to black children in the slums.

She had set up a dance class in the Cape Flats. For months she and her group practised to put on a performance in public. I simply had to attend the first night, which was also to be the last. That

Friday evening I set off on my own in a bus that took me to the 'non-white' suburbs. Soon we reached a part of town where the little houses began to look more and more like each other and the bus stops stood at greater distances apart. There were few street lights. After getting off the bus I began walking in search of the little hall. Turning a corner I came on a group of *skollies* – Cape Coloured toughs – who were having a go at each other. I took refuge behind a hedge. They had their jackets wrapped around their left arms as a kind of shield. Blades glittered in their right hands. The brawl was over in a moment. One of the figures lay where he had fallen.

I ran on as soon as the coast was clear. The impenetrable darkness notwithstanding, I did not dare to ask anyone the way to the hall. On getting there I found it to be packed with enthusiastic parents and relatives. I was the only white person present, I believe, but no one took any notice of me. The atmosphere was festive; first there was some singing, then came the performance. At the end of it I went up on the platform, in full view of everyone, and got from Susan the kiss I had for so long dreamed of.

A few months later, a year before our final examinations, her parents took her out of school. Her departure from the class was swift yet surrounded by queries, rumours, hypocritical silences. In all haste the family left for Australia.

It was around this time that I began to read the newspapers regularly. The *Cape Times* kept the score: every weekend about two hundred stabbing affrays took place around the city. We were – though no special notice was taken of the fact – entrapped in a kind of low-intensity civil war. Growing up here could only be thought of as a kind of mutilation.

It is impossible to describe how deep was the sense of mutual estrangement. Differences of language, faith or race were never more than the most obvious indicators of a chronic, irremediable lack of civil cohesion within the country as a whole. Little effort was made by most urban whites to cultivate any sense of common human decency. They had no idea that the social attitudes they took for granted had been learned: painstakingly inculcated and acquired. It is a mistake to imagine that they were brought up merely to discriminate against others on grounds of colour. The repulsion they felt was more profound. They had been taught to hate: a hate that gnawed at them like the hunger of an animal waiting to be fed.

I felt it too; but my own repugnance focused on everything that was white. During my final year at school I seldom went to a pub or party where my classmates would be found. All they ever did was bullshit about rugby matches or boast about their feats in the surf. Beachboys in the making. As soon as I was old enough to go about on my own, my inclinations drew me towards the inner city. There I found quite a different Africa from the one we were told about in the seclusion of the classroom. In the Muslim Upper Cape, on the slopes immediately above the downtown area, and in District Six, far from the teeny-boppers and the petty-bourgeois claustrophobia of the lily-white southern suburbs, there remained a world outside the crazy racial exclusions that bound our lives elsewhere.

At the age of eighteen I moved to Woodstock, close to District Six, a notoriously rundown area. For that very reason it felt freer than elsewhere; it was still the amorphous melting-pot by which

Verwoerd had felt so threatened in 1920. Racial integration had gone further here, and was more difficult to undo, than anywhere else. That it was a slum, a filthy and violent place, went without saying.

During the nineteenth century the population of District Six had consisted chiefly of liberated slaves, or their descendants, transported to the Cape from Java, Malaya and elsewhere by the Dutch East India Company. By the turn of the century they had been joined by immigrants and refugees from Europe, including about seven thousand Jews from the Baltic provinces of the Russian empire, British soldiers discharged at the end of the Anglo-Boer War, Boers bankrupted by that same war, black migrant labourers from the colony's eastern frontier. Ten or fifteen years later the district was regarded as a kind of transit zone: by which I mean that those who had succeeded moved away from it. The whites established themselves in the suburbs to the south of Table Mountain and along the coastline of Sea Point. This dispersal of population over the entire peninsula would have been impossible without the development of modern means of transport. The people who were left behind, within walking distance of the city centre, were dependent on employment in the harbour area and the factories around it. They were paid by the hour or day. When Verwoerd came to power the overwhelming majority of them were Coloured, a warning (to him) of the racial mixing that white poverty inevitably brought in its wake.

Alas, this area too was to be destroyed by the oppressive power of the state; not to speak of the constriction of the heart that was both pre-condition and consequence of government policy. District Six was regarded by the Nationalist Party as a 'black spot' (their term) disfiguring the fair forehead of the city. On 11 February 1966, the Minister for Community Affairs (their term, again) announced the end of District Six. There was to be no going back. It was to be completely flattened. The inhabitants would be driven en masse to the Cape Flats. They would have to manage there as best they could, far from their work, from the shelter of Table Mountain and from the streets once familiar to them. Dumped in a region tormented by dust and wind, they were left to their fate.

In the summer of 1966, after the murdered Verwoerd had been succeeded by a much feared former Minister of Justice named Balthasar Vorster, Demitrios Tsafendas was transferred from Robben Island to Pretoria Central Prison. He was placed in a cell next to death row and forgotten. Those who had hoped that the murder of Verwoerd might be followed by a popular revolt, or that such an event might shake the Afrikaners from their slumber, were shown to have been deceiving themselves. Dreamers all. Within the narrow coterie of their own kind, the whites clung to each other more closely than ever before. Any attempt at intercourse with the people with whom I had always felt myself most at ease – the Cape Coloureds – was automatically suspect in their eyes. I was frozen out, as were others like me.

If only I had been born black! What was left for me to look for, as a white?

Six months after the assassination I went into the consulate of the Netherlands, in Strand Street, and asked – in English – for a passport. They barely lifted their heads to look at me. Nor did they take notice of the fact that officially I had no existence in South

Africa. In order to escape compulsory military service, I had never registered for an identity document. I wandered around as best I could, paid no tax and carried no 'white pass'. The passport was issued forthwith.

I arrived in Europe in the spring of 1968. I had burned my boats behind me. I felt optimistic, wholly unprepared for the great thirst that awaited me, the nostalgia I would feel for the future I had left behind.

2   THE WAY BACK

How often, over the next twenty years, did I dream that I was back in South Africa? Euphoric dreams, they were, though always uncertain in their outcome.

I was woken in the morning by a radio quacking busily in Afrikaans. This was no dream. All night the notorious Cape south-easter had been blowing, shaking the window-frames with its great hands. I pulled the bedclothes aside, dressed hastily and made for the botanical gardens in the centre of town: the Company Gardens, as they are called, after the Dutch East India Company which had established the country's first white settlement here, directly under Table Mountain.

Were things still as they used to be? The trees were tenderly lit by a languid sun. Beneath the trees were some small tables. A dark-skinned man was mowing the grass. On the back of his orange overalls were the letters C.C.C. – Cape City Council. Surely no place on earth was pleasanter. Returning after so long an absence, I discovered, meant that I had to do everything all over again. I went through suburbs known to me, uphill and down: towards the mountain, through the city centre, down to the docks. I could have found my way around blindfold. The streets were empty; the sun's rays reached across to the booming sea. From a distance I could hear the call of the muezzin. I got on a double-decker bus going towards Sea Point. It too was empty. When we turned a corner, going away from the docks, there once more, where it had always been, yet seemingly brand-new too, was a service station with its petrol pumps. As the bus went by, the little building appeared to reconstruct itself from the past, so swiftly, yet complete in every detail.

In a lane next to it stood two people, a man and a woman. Both were in rags. The man's movements were slow but purposeful. With his clenched fist he struck the woman in the middle of her face. She fell, struggled upright and screamed soundlessly. He leaned towards her again, bending his head towards her breast. Then he pulled her blouse over her head and tore it in two. She crumpled against a wall. No passing car hooted. No one started towards her. It was as if a breeze had moved through some branches; nothing more.

Home again.

Later I took the train to the southern suburbs and the beaches of False Bay. It was not long since the signs on the station walls saying

'Whites Only' had been removed. Older yet brighter patches of ochre paint showed where those signs used to be. The train itself was still divided more or less along racial lines. The first-class coaches were mostly empty. Third class was packed. Second class did not exist. Coloureds and whites were to be found in first class; blacks on the bare wooden seats of third class.

We ambled through the southern suburbs. The window was open, letting in the warm air. Opposite me sat an elderly English-speaking woman, soft-skinned, smelling of lavender. She was visibly nervous. At every stop she breathed out with relief once it became clear that the noisy Cape Coloured throngs were rushing into the carriages behind us. The little station buildings, the fences and flowerbeds, looked orphaned, uncared-for, as if they had not been touched since my departure.

The crowds grew thicker as we left the white suburbs behind us. Now that racial segregation on the beaches had been abolished, the entire Coloured population of the Cape Flats seemed to be streaming towards sections of the coast previously forbidden to them. At Deep River station scores of youngsters ran jubilantly ahead of their parents. Every time the train began to move overexcited children sprinted alongside it, making daredevil attempts to get on board while their friends struggled to hold the sliding doors open for them. Of the conductor there was no sign.

On an impulse I got off the train at the bathing resort of Muizenberg. It had always struck me as a place with a certain British, colonial-style aspect. Now its British reticence had vanished. It was given over instead to what looked like a kind of carnival. An endlessly variegated crowd had taken possession of the beach. The families I had earlier seen rushing to board the train were complemented by all those who had made their way to the coast in clapped-out cars, minibuses and coaches.

I made my way along the promenade. Was all this true? Was I seeing right? Why had the old order lasted for so long? During the sixties a rigorous colour bar had been enforced here. If your skin looked too dark you could be told to take down your swimming trunks, so that the paleness or otherwise of your backside could be examined. At that time I'd hardly ever gone to this beach – not so much in protest against the rules and the ludicrous boundaries they protected, but because I felt such distaste for the Californian-style surfers putting on a display of their special kind of White Power. Now I wandered among thousands of people among whom I seemed to be the only one who may have reminded them of those distant White Power days.

How does one liberate a beach? This beach had been liberated.

In clothes of all styles and hues, as if taken from a children's dressing-up basket, the crowds sported in the water and along the promenade; they tumbled about on the grass and in the old-fashioned amusement park. They played soccer with tennis balls, cricket with bits of driftwood; they dragged fishing boats out of the waves, boasted and shouted over the catch, bargained and argued. The air was heavy and sultry. Gulls veered and hung in a breeze smelling strongly of seaweed. I walked back and forth, fascinated by the animation around me, the noise, the sense I had of how ordinary was the appearance of things that for so long had been unthinkable.

Many of the older people wore white hats, shawls and white, crocheted fezzes. Most of the youngsters had been born since my departure from the country. I did not see a single face known to me, yet everywhere I recognised the familiar 'Malay' features and Arabian eyes of people who had been driven without apology out of 'our' suburbs. And here I was in the middle of them all: ghost-pale, long-nosed, tremulous as a hare.

Within a matter of days I had begun working in the National Library – an imposing edifice, a replica of the Fitzwilliam Museum in Cambridge – which stands near the parliamentary buildings, the Supreme Court, the once dreaded police headquarters on Caledon Square, and the Anglican Cathedral. I had by then paid my inevitable visits to what used to be my family home, as well as to the factory in which my father had worked as an instrument-maker. I had also succeeded in getting myself mugged twice: the first time on coming out of an ebulliently low-life disco ('The Base') at about three in the morning; the second time, more frighteningly, in a train, in broad daylight, and at the point of a knife. 'We only want your money, man,' explained the child who held the blade directly to my stomach. He and his mates were all children, long-legged children with muddy eyes and fuzz on their cheek-bones. I pulled a few crumpled notes out of my pocket, but they were not to be so easily satisfied. 'We *really* want your money, man,' hissed the knife-carrier, gesturing at my navel with his weapon. I began to disgorge everything I had in my pockets. Coins bounced about on the floor. A general scrabbling, grabbing and swearing followed. The people in the neighbouring sections of the carriage did not move. It all seemed to go on for an eternity. Then came a change in the rhythm of the train, the sound of brakes, a flickering of light and shadow. We were entering Salt River station.

Doors opened noisily. My besiegers turned, hesitated and made off down the platform. What I most wanted to do was to light a cigarette. But they had taken my matches too.

Later, in a dimly lit office in the city's main station, I reported the incident to the railway police. I did not understand why I went to the trouble of doing it. For the sake of the statistics? '*Yirra*, those blerrie buggers!' said the policeman to whom I told my tale. 'Why don't you carry a gun?'

From that world, from the world outside, the library hardly offered me a refuge. Each time I entered it I remembered how impressed I had been when I first visited the place as a seventeen-year-old matriculant. Its lofty cupola, which seemed to float in mid-air when you looked up at it, served in effect as a whispering gallery or echo-chamber. The turn of a page, the faintest murmur, was transformed into an unforgiving crackle. A cough was like rifle-shot. Sitting there, pretending to be an adult, I would concentrate on keeping as still as I could, lest I disturb the others. Now, in another chamber, I bent for days on end over card indexes and copies of newspapers preserved on microfiche, scavenging and gathering material by instinct, basketsful of material, hoping that I might find a use for it all – though I could not imagine what that use might turn out to be. What would I do with the 'Report of the Commission of Enquiry into Secret Organisations' (1965)? Or a study entitled *Possession by Spirits among the Zulus*? Or the newspaper cutting headed 'Bantus [i.e. Africans] to be Greeted in their Own Manner' (1966), which carried an authoritative ruling from central government that white civil servants were in no circumstances ever to shake hands with blacks?

The past unfolded before me incoherently, yet in a manner which swept away all rationalisations. 'You knew it was happening, you read these same newspapers and heard the rumours, didn't you?' Thus I reproached myself. Again and again the ugliness of that period thrust itself into my consciousness: the stupidity, the lies, the violence, the censorship – from the massacre at Sharpeville in 1960 and even before then too: the grotesquely obscene political and 'immorality' trials, the Dutch Reformed dominees trapped in garages with their Coloured maids, the farmers spied on in the open veld with their female domestics and duly brought to reckoning before the courts. With a rising gorge I deliberately made my way through a four months' sampling of issues of *Die Burger*, the Nationalist Party daily newspaper in the Cape, from 1 January 1960 to the end of April: one hundred and twenty days under Verwoerd's premiership, chosen more or less at random. What I found there was a caricature of a country, my country, sick, disordered, petrified.

From time to time, fleeing from the nauseating facts I was dredging up, I would go out into the Company Gardens. Or I would sit on the terrace and drink tea, trying to contain my anger. Seagulls raised their cries among the magnolias. Table Mountain was always visible through the leaves of the trees. More than a thousand metres high, too broad to look around, it was a theatrical yet ever silent witness of what passed below. So many important events in South African history had taken place in this precinct: demonstrations, marches, processions.

Murder too. Among all the other documents awaiting me was the 'Report of the Commission of Enquiry into the Death of the Late Honourable Dr Hendrik Frensch Verwoerd' (1966), which gave an account of the assassination, together with the official and (supposedly) final version of the life of Demitrios Tsafendas. I paid my money and carried away a photocopy of the report in its entirety. I had no idea then how extensive and how revealing was the material about Tsafendas which I would find elsewhere. Nor did I guess that seven years later, after several further visits to the country and many bureaucratic delays, I would at last be allowed to come face to face with him.

3 THE BASTARD

BORN IN 1918, Demitrios Tsafendas could remember nothing of the first house and garden he had lived in, on the Rua Andrade Corvo in Lourenço Marques (now Maputo). He spent no more than a year there.

His father, Michaelis Tsafandakis, who was Cretan by birth, had migrated from the Egyptian port of Alexandria to the highveld city of Pretoria in the Transvaal. Early in 1916 he moved to Mozambique to take a job with an Italian firm of marine engineers. He was a striking young man with a heavy moustache and a lengthy stride; like an ostrich's, some said. He soon won a reputation as a hardworking but excitable man. The Africans who worked under him looked on him with some fear. Within the local Greek community he was respected for his independence of mind. People put his brusque, inflammable temperament down to his Cretan origins. That he employed two black maids in his house on Rua Andrade excited no particular comment. With one of them – the seventeen-year-old Amelia Williams – he shared his bed. She was a girl of mixed European and African descent. In the tropics it was more or less the order of the day for a single man to keep a concubine. Everyone assumed that Michaelis would eventually marry a fellow Greek.

The house was semi-detached. The neighbours saw Amelia going about her chores and working in the garden. She watered and fed the chickens, humming with a strange intensity as she did so. She went barefoot and wore a multi-coloured cotton skirt like that worn by the women in neighbouring Swaziland. Over her shoulders she wore a light shawl. The rumour was that Michaelis had his hands full keeping her under control.

In 1917 she fell pregnant. She spent some time with her family in Namaacha, a district on the border between Mozambique and Swaziland. She returned in midsummer. In January she gave birth to a boy.

Michaelis was confronted by a dilemma. The child was his first-born son, but marriage with Amelia was out of the question. He allowed the child to be registered in his name in the office of the local Administraçao Civil. The entry reads: 'Demitrios, 14 January 1918, son of Amelia Williams and Miguel Tsafandakis.' Some months later an Orthodox priest was brought down from Johannesburg to baptise Demitrios. His godfather – Michaelis's good friend Perandonakis, also a Cretan – bore the costs of the ceremony. Amelia did not attend it. By then relations between her and Michaelis had been severed.

The house next door was occupied by Anthony Maw who later became honorary consul for Greece in Lourenço Marques. After Amelia Williams's departure Maw and his wife wondered how their neighbour would cope. The baby was unmistakably a half-blood. For the young English couple this meant that he was bound to become a shackle around his father's legs; but they kept their opinion to themselves. In effect the baby was being brought up by the servant girl.

One day in spring Maw leaned over the hedge that divided the two gardens. He could see the maid sitting among the bougainvilleas with the baby on her lap. The father stood nearby. Tsafandakis – who had always been on the sturdy side – had grown stout. The two men fell into conversation. Michaelis spoke English only hesitantly, sometimes in cryptic fashion. In three months' time he would turn thirty-five, he confided to his neighbour. His family, which still lived in Crete and in Egypt, was in the process of seriously searching for a bride for him. Maw remarked that a young European wife would not find it agreeable to be burdened with an illegitimate child of that kind. After some roundabout palaver Michaelis confessed that he wanted to send his little son to Alexandria. There he could be brought up by Michaelis's mother. The problem was that he did not know anyone who would be able to accompany the weanling to Egypt.

By this time Maw's wife had joined in the conversation. It so happened that she knew someone who would shortly be going to

Athens. By steamship, through the Suez Canal. She promised to find out about it.

Among the Greeks this was quite a common way of dealing with such matters. Many grandparents in effect brought up their grandchildren.

The widow Katerina Tsafandakis fetched her grandson Demitrios from the boat in Port Said. He was to spend his next six years in Alexandria. That is to say: his earliest memories were of the cosmopolitan cultural life of the eastern Mediterranean. At home he spoke Greek; in the street, Arabic. His first impressions were coloured by Mediterranean light, a confusion of warehouses and bazaars, the heat and crowds of the small lanes near the docks. The great commercial city looked at the same time east and west; though one window was open on the unstable world of the Levant, the city still lay within the British sphere of influence, and its closely knit Greek colony dated back to ancient times.

Katerina lived on the top storey of a house on Rue Toussoum Pasha, not far from the pale-red building of the Banco di Roma. Around the corner was Place Mohammed Ali, the biggest square in the town centre, where the colonial court buildings and the cotton exchange were to be found. Towards evening the noisy chatter of the Alexandrian sparrows could be heard from the trees. The sparrows, which landed in great numbers on the terrace of the house, fascinated Demitrios from an early age. During the hot summers he slept on the terrace and closed his eyes to the rustle of the birds. In the mornings, at first light, he was woken by the voice of the imam, carried from the mosque all over the suburb.

Grandmother Tsafandakis gave him the pet name Mimis. She

took him with her to the market, to the Anglican church in the Place Mohammed Ali and the cathedral of St Saba, the seat of the Orthodox patriarch. Later she took him to the English puppet theatre in the city, which was particularly popular among Greek children. For the rest he would spend the whole day dressed in a trailing jellaba, playing at being a little Arab boy.

From his grandmother the little boy learned to identify the electric trams which ran in a elaborate network all over the city. Mimis surprised her by the quickness with which he learned to recognise the different services. He pointed out to her their symbols: the green lozenge which marked the tramline to the south, the red half-moon of the Ragheb Pasha line, the white star, red circle and green leaf of the other lines.

Sometimes Katerina worried over her grandson. He was seldom ill-behaved but often she thought him too withdrawn. He was uneasy with children of his own age and kept to himself. She stuffed him with sultanas, raisins and dates, which he loved.

His father visited Egypt a few times. The sea route along the coast of East Africa was much frequented and Michaelis's contacts with Greek shipowners made such journeys easy to arrange. Mimis looked forward to these visits though they were too irregular for him to get to know his father. The little presents he received from him he found strange: wood carvings of an unfamiliar kind, a little hand-held thumb piano made out of a gourd, with keys of bent steel.

By this time Michaelis was a married man. The young Marika, who had come to him from the Greek community in Port Said, accompanied him on these journeys. As Demitrios grew up, he began to look on Marika as his mother: a mother at a distance. In remote Lourenço Marques he eventually acquired from her a little sister and brother – Evangelina and Victor. But the children remained mere names to him and Lourenço Marques was a phantom, a dream town found only in stories.

Mimis had to go on living with Katerina.

When he could not fall asleep she would recite to him long passages from the *Erotokritas*, an epic that she knew by heart, just as the Muslim youngsters could recite from the Koran for an hour at a time.

They lay together on the sofa next to the open window. The evenings were smoky and restless. The Cretan verses comforted him like candy.

There were questions the child could not ask her but of whose nature he was fully aware. Demitrios had the feeling that something was being kept from him. For reasons he could not understand he was at a disadvantage. The circumstances of his birth remained unspoken about, unknown to him.

By the time he was seven years old he was a quiet but outwardly contented boy. He was free to wander as he wished through the town. He rambled about the docks, attracted by their hubbub and by the ships on their way to Tripoli or Heraklion. He spent the midday hours on the Corniche, the broad road along the coast from which you could see the fort on Qayt Bay. It was the only trace of the ancient lighthouse still standing, or so Katerina had once told him. In the Greek quarter of the town, behind St Saba's Cathedral, Mimis was a well-known figure. Only Ras el Tin was forbidden territory, the Turkish district near the Cape of Figs. Disorder was brewing there.

The uprising of the Arabs against the British regime made a great impression on him. All the doors of the house were bolted. There were riots in his street. The nationalists set fire to the covered market where he bought his sherbets. From the terrace of his house he looked down on the English and Australian troops as they formed up and suddenly opened fire. With salvo upon salvo they drove the rebels out of the district. When his grandmother saw him sitting there she dragged him roughly indoors. It was the only time he could remember hearing her curse.

By 1925 Katerina had grown too frail to look after him. Mimis had become too much of a handful for her. In the course of that year his father arrived. The plan was that he would take the boy south, back to the promised land of Lourenço Marques. Mimis had grown into a slender youngster, with a narrow face surmounted by an uncontrollable bush of crinkled hair.

Things had gone well with Michaelis, whose family, for some time resident in the Britannia Hotel, was now living in an apartment on the top storey of a large, whitewashed building in a pleasant part of town, on 24 July Avenue. In it there would be enough room for them all: for Marika, Michaelis and their two children, Evangelina and Victor. Another girl, Helena, soon followed. Michaelis wished to do his best for Mimis, too. He had to go to school and learn the local languages. Marika had objected to his arrival, but she had been overborne. The domestic staff was expanded to include an extra maid. For the eight-year-old Demitrios it was difficult at first to accept the change from a Mediterranean to an African style of life. He could understand nobody outside the family. He missed the familiar sounds and the comfortable neighbourhood of his grandmother's house. He was sent to school in a Portuguese mission in the city and was placed among the children in the lowest grade. The white children spoke in a harsh, bitten-off manner, as if giving orders. The blacks shouted. Even nature and natural events seemed loud and abrupt here. In the evenings it looked as if the sun died in a single moment behind the hills. In the mornings it stood up as if with a clap above the horizon. There was no sense of intermediacy, no dawn or dusk.

This absence of nuance was visible everywhere. In Alexandria the Greeks were a respected minority, protected by the British, even after Egypt had declared itself independent in 1922. Here, below the equator, prejudices were much sharper. The Anglo-Saxon and Portuguese way of doing things emphasised distinctions within the colony. Race and class reinforced each other. The Greek merchants, tobacco planters and workers were looked down on, along with 'coolies and local savages'. The Greeks in Mozambique clung together in their own community, seeking to preserve what they could of the culture of their motherland. Michaelis Tsafandakis knew less about local politics than he did about developments in Athens. And in general he was less well informed and educated than his wife.

Demitrios was not a part of his father's milieu, but then where did he really belong? In his new surroundings he missed the intimacy, warmth and mutual trust which he had enjoyed with Katerina. Whether or not he would ever be able to fit in would depend largely on Marika.

She was an intelligent woman, born to a worldly family in Port Said. Next to the corpulent Michaelis, she looked small, with an athletic figure and an urgent way of going about things. She had a pockmarked but agreeable face. A thick plait hung down almost to her waist. She spoke French and a little Italian and had rapidly learned Portuguese and English. At the time of Demitrios's arrival she was just twenty-three years old, seventeen years younger than her husband.

In her heart she looked on Michaelis's love-child as an intruder and feared that his father would favour him above her own children. Nevertheless she had decided to treat him no differently from the others. It was clear to her that Demitrios had to be taken in hand. He could not read or write, he knew nothing of Greek history. He seemed to have been left to his own devices in Egypt.

Mimis soon came to admire his new mother. Even if she remained somewhat distant in manner, she gave him treats from her kitchen and was good at telling stories. She told him about De Lesseps and the building of the Suez Canal, about the Acropolis and the Orthodox saints. After dinner she would bring thick books to the table and read to the children. She had a gramophone on which she played European records. And what perhaps impressed him most about her was that she had set up a small shrine in an alcove near the bedrooms. (There was no Greek Orthodox church in Lourenço Marques.) The family paid a formal visit to that confined, darkened space last thing at night, every night. Little oil-lamps she had brought with her from Port Said remained alight twenty-four hours a day.

The flames threw a wonderful scintillation over the icons. It kept alive in Demitrios's mind the places he used to visit with his grandmother in his Alexandrian days. Evening after evening the chilly golden saints and fathers of the church stared flickeringly down at him. It was as if the air itself was aflame, while preserving an eternal coolness of its own.

Outside, the heat was overwhelming. For six months or longer Marika stood by her resolution not to make a distinction between her children and the newcomer; then, all at once, it shattered. It was clear to her that Michaelis had become greatly attached to the boy; even more so than she had feared. He gave much less of his attention to the younger children. And then there was the climate! She complained that her head of hair was much too heavy to bear. She wanted to cut it short, because she suffered from severe, recurring headaches, especially now, in the summer. It was as if her skull was being constantly pulled at. But Michaelis forbade her to cut her hair. Sometimes he could behave tyrannically towards her.

'Your son has been messing about with your things,' she would call out maliciously to him. *Your* son.

Mimis was a nuisance, a burden to her. He disrupted the harmonious life of the family. Evangelina and little Victor, especially, suffered under his teasing and changes of mood. Punishing him did not help. When Michaelis rebuked him he would sit in the kitchen and stare silently in front of him. Or he would fall into a rage. Outside the house he was treated like some kind of primitive. And he behaved like one too: unpredictable and threatening.

After a further six months, the rows between him and Marika were a daily occurrence. Michaelis found their quarrelling insufferable. When Mimis turned nine he was sent to a boarding school for white, English-speaking children in the Union of South Africa.

Many children from middle-class families of continental European background went to such places and managed well enough. The educational system in the Transvaal was more developed than anything to be found in the Portuguese colony. His command of English would no doubt soon improve.

So, for the first time in his life, Mimis found himself living far from the coast and the smell of the sea. The bleak little Transvaal town of Middelburg lay four hundred kilometres west of Lourenço Marques and about a hundred kilometres east of Pretoria.

He was placed in Nelson House Hostel, a large, elongated, colonial-style building, with a shady verandah and a neglected garden in front of it. The pupils in this hostel came almost exclusively from Greek and Portuguese families, a group that was kept together partly but not entirely because of their backwardness in English. On their arrival, all students of foreign background were put back a year or two in class. Stimulated by the differences in life style between themselves and the other boys, they developed a camaraderie of their own. They also had the advantage of being able to speak in secret tongues, and they generally did well in all subjects other than English and Afrikaans. For this they were duly persecuted by the other boys. Everyone looked askance at them. The prejudices of the English-speaking townsfolk ran no less deeply than those of the local Afrikaners. The Portuguese were called 'sea-kaffirs'; the Greeks were notorious for being untrustworthy. The whites whispered among themselves about the dark practices that went on in the hostel.

'We all knew,' one of the Afrikaans-speaking boys from another hostel later recalled, 'that sodomy was a common habit in that tightly knit group.'

Demitrios was in the same position as the others from Mozambique, and this created a bond between them and him. If he was noticed at all in this group, initially, it was because of the seriousness of his manner. He was strikingly earnest for a boy of his age. Another burden on him was the frequent feverish attacks he suffered. No enquiry was made into the possibility that these might have been malarial in origin. It was evident that he believed himself to be out of the ordinary. He would speak in a joking, offhand manner to one of the women teachers about his life in Egypt. Later his feelings about the school grew darker. Its ethos stuck in his throat. British ways were stricter and more heavy-handed than those he had known before, either from his father or his grandmother. He was compelled to take part in sports like cricket and athletics of which he understood nothing. If he felt homesick it was not so much for his parents as for his racially mixed companions at the mission school in Lourenço Marques. He missed particularly the voices of the black children. He missed Marika's kitchenmaid. The food in the hostel was unpalatable to him: sausages, kippers, oatmeal with too little sugar, mealie meal porridge.

His greatest pleasure was to go to the automatic sweets-machine outside Cleggs Cafe in the *dorp*'s main street. Each time he was given his pocket money by Mr Martindale, the warden of the hostel, he went straight to Cleggs. He fed the machine with the giant, British-style copper pennies in use then, with the date of their minting stamped on them: 1921, 1899, 1909. Then the candies came out and he rolled them in his hand.

'Very good. Remarkably good.'

That was how he felt then, with his mouth full of chocolate. That was how, a lifetime later – after asking me if I happened to have any chocolate with me – he chose to describe the taste to me.

After a couple of terms in the Transvaal his command of English was still limited, but he could speak it freely enough. At the age of twelve or thirteen Mimis was familiar with five languages, but he could speak none of them correctly. His Arabic lay in the past. The same was true of Shangaan, the local African language, which he had learned from the mission-school children. He disliked Afrikaans (South African Dutch) which struck him as a language appropriate to the country: one of naked, stony sounds. In Middelburg he dreamed in Greek and woke in English.

By the time he reached the fifth grade in the school he had become the clown of his peer group, more because of his wild gesticulations than because of anything he said. When he sang Cretan songs at school concerts, he had the excited, laughing, applauding audience eating out of his hand. Yet his gesturing and general appearance also provoked the other boys to tease and bully him. He was plagued especially by a boy named Benjamin Levy, whose father was the manager of the Savoy Hotel in Lourenço Marques. On one occasion the fat Benny, together with friend Sammy Schmahmann, kicked him on the shins in the wasteland beyond the playing fields. Mimis struck back at them vainly, and came away with a bloody nose.

This was the first time that he heard the expression 'Coloured' being flung at him.

'You're nothing but a lousy Coloured!' shouted the fat boy. 'A lousy bloody Coloured.'

He at once felt ashamed and humiliated, though he did not

know why. Boer, Briton, Jew, Coloured – these distinctions had largely passed him by. His parents were Greek: could there be anything surprising, then, if his skin was darker than that of the pale, English-speaking ghosts of the highveld? Nor was Mimis the only boy with crinkly hair in Middelburg Primary School. But there was no one else whose words were so twisted and strange. His boasts were always exposed, his fantasies convinced nobody. Whenever he told lies or tried to cheat at games the others saw through him at once. Only in eating and in singing did he distinguish himself – the intensity with which he flung himself into both these activities was beyond measure.

In the hills outside the little town he had discovered some caves. It was a primitive and isolated place, surrounded by strangely formed boulders, some the work of nature, some of men's hands. He spent hours in these caves. Alone. With a candle. Though no icons were to be found there, the place was his shrine.

Twice a year, during the school holidays, he went home by rail: for a couple of weeks in the winter and for almost two months in the summer. Marika was happier to see him go than to see him come. In September 1928 she had had another girl, who was baptised Katerina, in honour of the child's grandmother Tsafandakis. In addition to the three girls, Marika had her son Victor, who was often unwell, to look after. Each time her stepson appeared she became more and more convinced that there was something abnormal about him. He was always acting, putting on a performance the whole time. When he thought no one was watching him he would pull crazy faces. The full story about Amelia was still hidden from Demitrios, but Marika was not surprised to hear that he was accused by the boys at his school of being a Coloured. It would have been better for him, she thought, if he had remained in Egypt. In Egypt he would have 'passed' more easily.

Demitrios spent much of his time in the kitchen. He had no real relationship with the other children, his three-year-old sister aside. Sometimes he would go into Evangelina's bedroom. He called her Betty Boop, after the little girl in the American strip cartoon. He explained to Betty Boop how gunpowder worked, and told her he was going to make skyrockets with it. Evangelina understood little of what he was saying, but she enjoyed listening to him. Her brother used words that were strange to her. He spoke of 'tuck' when he meant sweets and crisps; he called bananas 'lady's fingers', and brought a bunch of small bananas from the kitchen to show her what a good name this was for them.

His father too was unhappy with the boy's appearance and demeanour. He asked himself why Demitrios was so timid and turned in on himself; so chicken-breasted, skinny, weedy. He had round, girlish shoulders, and showed no interest in the activities that kept the other youngsters in the neighbourhood busy. At home he was under everyone's feet; when Michaelis took him to his workplace, at the firm of Vucellato, he usually just followed his father about. He did like watching the welders at work; then he would lose interest. He collected strips of metal from the lathes, played with grindstones and moulds.

Michaelis discussed the boy with an old acquaintance, Guilliema Conte, who had set up a gym in the city. Senõr Conte offered to take the youngster under his wing during the summer months. Demitrios, he said, should learn to box. Then at least he would be able to defend himself if anyone ever called him a 'blackie' back in Middelburg. In subsequent years Mimis went fairly often to the gymnasium set up by Conte and his brother; at first in order to oblige his father, later because he became interested in the sport.

Jack Dempsey was soon one of his greatest heroes. The other was Buster Keaton.

At the beginning of the nineteen thirties the world-wide depression dominated life in southern Africa. Michaelis did not know if he would be able to survive in Mozambique, or how he would be able to pay Mimis's fees at the boarding school in Middelburg. Maritime traffic had dwindled. The firm for which he worked was going downhill. Many immigrants to Portuguese East Africa were leaving for the Transvaal, where conditions were a little better. In 1931 Michaelis applied to the South African Department of Immigration and Asiatic Affairs (*sic*) for permission for the children, at least, to be registered as members of the Greek community in Pretoria.

In that summer Demitrios returned once again to the family residence in 24 July Avenue. After four years in Middelburg he had got no further than the sixth grade. The next eighteen months he spent as a student, supposedly, at the Portuguese mission school which he had attended before.

For the most part he simply played truant; he spent his days wherever his fancy took him. At night he rummaged around the apartment. Marika found it hard to cope with his appetite. He ate as much as he could, whenever he could; yet he remained as thin as ever. Was that usual for a boy of his age? She did not know. The only thing he really cared for was the gramophone. He said he wanted to learn the piano, but there was no money to buy such a thing for him. He sat with red-rimmed eyes in the front room of the apartment, doing nothing. She went to her brother, who had been living in the neighbourhood for the last few years, for advice. He told her that Demitrios was a loafer; the trouble with him was that he had never been properly disciplined. Marika's sister, Anna, who had married a Greek wrestler and also settled in Lourenço Marques, said the exact opposite. They should let the youngster alone.

In his own haphazard fashion Demitrios explored the various quarters of Lourenço Marques, the docks, the outlying slums to the north. He liked to visit Gregoris, who supplied the whole town with ice cream. The cold storage abutted on a house with many rooms. In one of them he got to know Cora, a woman who wore nail varnish of a different colour every time he visited her; she was a Portuguese or possibly a Coloured. He also liked to hang about in the Akropolis, the large, modern department store in the centre of town, where everything was spread out for inspection. In the evenings he visited the Contes' gym, where they called him 'Skinny'. He boxed featherweight, flailing his arms wildly in the ring. No one took him seriously as a contender. He didn't have it in him.

One afternoon he lay in bed with Betty Boop. No one else was at home. The two of them had taken off nearly all their clothes, but it was not clear to him who had taken the initiative in doing this. Mimis stroked her shoulder.

*

After the murder of Verwoerd, Tsafendas was questioned for days at a time by the security police. Several times they went over the story of his life. On a Monday morning, 12 September 1966, he said that he had forgotten to tell them something important the previous night. What he then declared threw a startlingly different light on the unhappy relations within the family between 1925 and 1927, when he had first been sent away to school – and indeed subsequently. His stepmother, he said, had abused him. Because he was heir to his father's property, Marika had turned the whole family against him. She was determined to destroy his 'masculine qualities'. Having used that unusual phrase, Demitrios followed it with another. She began, he said, 'to *corrupt* me'. He felt that he had been spoiled and defiled. Even before his departure for Middelburg she had persuaded her brother to rape him.

'My uncle dragged me into a room and committed an unnatural deed with me. I got very scared. I was just a child.'

It sounded as if he had grabbed the story out of thin air. It appeared to have been put together out of tales from the experiences of others, or from events that had happened earlier or later in his life. Demitrios looked at his past as if through a kaleidoscope – depending on need or desire, he would give it a quarter-turn this way or that.

He regarded the period 1934–35, after he had left the school in Middelburg and was living again in Lourenço Marques, as the most painful he ever went through. In retrospect he felt it was then that he had been most vulnerable to what he called 'corruption'. It was then, he insisted, that his view of himself and of the world at large had darkened and hardened irrevocably.

*

Of the hiding given to him by his father, when he came home and found Mimis and Betty Boop in bed together, Demitrios could remember little, except that he had lost consciousness: or rather, that he had come around while the Portuguese doctor was attending to him. His aunt Anna was trying to calm Marika. For many days afterwards she would not address a single word to him. During this time Michaelis simply stayed away from the house. Demitrios could not understand why his father had attacked him so violently. Evangelina and he often lay on top of one another, in the garden too – tickling each other, playing leapfrog, carrying on like crazy people. Sometimes they pretended that her bed was a boat. Betty Boop was by far his best friend in the family.

He was kept out of school; not as a punishment but because after that episode he began to be overcome by attacks of uncontrollable rage. His parents were afraid of what he might do to the other pupils. He refused to eat for a week and they could do nothing but again call the doctor to come and see him. He was left with a bottle of tonic of which he was to drink a tablespoon a day until he felt better. The doctor recommended exposure to sunlight too. Every day he was to spend such and such a period in the sun. After a month of this treatment he was almost as dark as an African. He refused to go back to the mission school, even when he himself declared that he now felt much better. Finally they arrived at a compromise. Mimis would now go to evening classes at an English-language institution in the town.

Michaelis Tsafandakis eventually came to the decision that he no longer had a future in Mozambique. The family should move to Pretoria as soon as possible. He would go ahead, to find a job and a place for the family to live in. Marika would follow with the three children. And Demitrios? The ambitions that Michaelis had once nourished for him were by now much moderated; his erratic behaviour forbade them. It was clear that he would never become an engineer of any kind like his father. Given the state of race relations in South Africa it would probably be better for him to remain in Lourenço Marques. Talking to the Greek owner of the Akropolis, Mr Sideris, Michaelis suggested that a place might be found for the boy in the store – possibly in the kiosk selling books and magazines.

Mimis saw little of his father in the months before the departure of the family. Nothing Michaelis said to him assuaged his conviction that he was being abandoned. Even his stepmother suddenly seemed to be more concerned about how he would manage in the future than Michaelis, the man who had previously been the most important figure in his life.

In the late summer of 1935 Marika saw to it that a medicine against tapeworms, prescribed by the Portuguese doctor he had been seeing, was administered to Mimis. On one of the succeeding days, to Marika's surprise and relief, a worm two or three feet long was found in his stools. That was the explanation, presumably, of his underfed appearance.

Mimis wanted to take the entire stool to the doctor, so that it could be investigated. Had he not promised he would do so? He also wanted to be certain that the head of the creature did not remain in his bowels. But, ignoring his protests, Marika washed the entire mess down the WC. Too late, she realised how much importance he had attached to it. On hearing what she had done he rushed into the kitchen and began hammering on the dresser with his fist – hammering and hammering. When he paused for a moment Marika gave him money and told him to buy an ice cream with it. He turned around and threw the coins out of the window. What did she think he was – a child?

Mimis felt as if a door had been slammed shut in front of him. Left behind in Lourenço Marques, he no longer had any obligations to the family and could do whatever he wished. He regarded Marika's assurance that he would always be welcome in Pretoria as nothing more than hypocrisy. They were glad to be rid of him. In August 1935 he asked for permission from the South African Interior Ministry to enter the country. It would be a formality, he thought. Five months later he received a note telling him that his application had been refused.

Mimis was bitterly disappointed – and suspicious. The South African consulate in Lourenço Marques would not discuss the matter further. Also: why was he suddenly held in such disregard by the local Greek community? His step-uncle, Marika's brother, would have nothing to do with him. In any case this uncle was on the point of leaving for Rhodesia, where he planned to become a tobacco farmer. Mr Sideris (for whom Mimis now sorted newspapers, arranged the books in the kiosk and helped with the cash sales) allowed him to take back to his little flat each day a free copy of the *Lourenço Marques Guardian*. But it was clear that Mrs Sideris did not want him to come near her house. Was she afraid for her daughters? He was now seventeen years old, a head taller than her husband, taller than his own father.

Mimis could not let the matter rest. The Sideris girls were pretty, like pictures. With their pale, oval faces and black hair they reminded him – or so he liked to believe – of the girls of Alexandria.

He did not know his place. When he made an unannounced visit to the Sideris house and, omitting the usual greetings in Greek, went straight to the gramophone, Mrs Sideris took him up abruptly.

'You're just like your mother,' she shouted at him.

He gazed at her in astonishment.

'Your mother, your real mother, was a black, a Coloured woman. A mulatto,' she repeated, in Portuguese.

He heard her, all right; but he regarded what she had said as just another of the many obscure insults or accusations he had shaken off before. He was a Greek, the son of a Greek, the grandson of a Greek. He left the house without replying to her. The following day, however, he went to the office of the Administraçao Civil. He looked up the records there, and for the first time in his life read the name of his mother: Amelia Williams. She had died nine years previously, in one of the 'native' areas of Lourenço Marques: on 12 January 1927, two days before his ninth birthday. Someone in the office confirmed for him that she was a Coloured, of part-Swazi origins.

Suddenly he had to think of himself in two parts, as a kind of double: one half this, the other that; half *non-white*, the other half . . . acceptable. In South Africa 'White' and 'Swazi' were written with capital letters, as if they referred to nations; 'mulatto' and 'bastard' with small letters, for such people were without consequence; they had come from nowhere and would amount to nothing. He listened to the fan going around and around, just below the ceiling of his room. Who then were his grandparents?

He returned to the Administraçao Civil, and went from office to office seeking information which might be relevant to him, but came out with nothing. One file said that Amelia Williams had a German father; another that her father was English. No one could tell him where she was buried.

For the eighteen-year-old Tsafendas everything he had always felt to be suspect or ominous about himself now fell into place. His close-packed, curly hair. His skin colour – which he had previously thought of as Mediterranean. Grandmother Tsafendas's vagueness whenever he asked her about his mother. The resentment and hostility of Marika and the contempt towards him shown by his uncle. The teasing at school. The negative reply from the South African immigration service. The tentative, curious glances constantly thrown at him; the indefinable hesitation with which people greeted him.

In one blow he had become other to himself, irrevocably. He now knew himself to be literally and figuratively the black sheep of the family. And the authorities in the neighbouring country, South Africa, knew all about him too.

However, he did not abandon his hopes of joining his family there. By this time Michaelis was working as a welder for the state-owned Iron and Steel Corporation (ISCOR). Again Mimis applied for permission to enter the country; again the consulate in Lourenço Marques reported that it would not be granted to him.

He consoled himself as best he could with Cora, the woman with painted nails, who lived in the house of many rooms.

4   ADRIFT WITHOUT ANCHOR

OF ALL FOODS Demitrios most loved lobster. He told me so, with much emphasis, when I visited him for the first time in the psychiatric institution in the Transvaal in which he had long been incarcerated. The giant crabs which his stepmother had served up in Lourenço Marques were splendid too. But nothing could beat lobster or langoustine.

'The best food I ever ate, lobster.'

The attendant in the ward, a hefty man in a white coat who happened to be passing at that moment, turned to us with a grimace. 'Lobster? What's lobster?' and before we could answer let the door to the kitchen bang shut behind him.

People in the interior of the country are often suspicious of seafood. Creatures that live in their shells are thought to be disgusting: impure somehow.

As a schoolboy Demitrios had made the journey between Mozambique and the Transvaal at least a dozen times, travelling uncomfortably in the steam train that connected the coastline on the Indian Ocean with the great plateau, two thousand metres higher, which is the heartland of South Africa. In 1936 he decided that he would follow his family to Pretoria, despite the refusal of the authorities to give him a visa to enter the country. He knew just how porous, how poorly controlled, were the borders. In the autumn of that year he concealed himself among some machinery packed in a railway goods-wagon, and crossed the border at Komatipoort with no difficulty. Then on to Pretoria.

For some time after his arrival he worked in the Fountains Cafe, not far from the railway station. He scrubbed tables and ran about the streets on errands, often with a tray in his hand. For the first but not for the last time in his career he was living as an illegal immigrant, someone who had slipped through officaldom's nets. On the Witwatersrand – the sprawling metropolis of Johannesburg and its surroundings – there were many thousands of others in the same position. The depression of the previous few years had coincided with a severe drought on the highveld. Needy farmers, both white and black, as well as poverty-stricken families from the neighbouring Portuguese and British colonies, streamed towards the city. Most of them would never return to the rural areas from which they had come. The struggle for existence among these newcomers was inevitably fought out on racial lines, and hence on unequal terms. The whites had the vote; and their representatives in parliament passed law after law to protect their constituents against competition from the blacks.

Demitrios had not been warmly received by his family in Pretoria. His brother Victor now regarded himself as the oldest son and Marika encouraged him to do so. Contact between Demitrios and the others was seldom pleasant. Within two months he had moved to Hillbrow, a suburb of Johannesburg not far from the centre of the city. There he went from one petty job to another, most of them in the catering trade. From the City Tearoom to the Elgin Cafe in Jeppe Street and from there to the Cosmopolitan Restaurant.

He was almost nineteen years old. His employers found him friendly enough, though also touchy sometimes. Those who got to know him better thought him talkative, intelligent, given to day-dreaming. While on his own in Lourenço Marques he had changed, turned some kind of a corner. The introverted, hollow-chested pubescent had become a rough, loquacious young man who was proud of the languages he knew and of the ideas he could express in all of them. He read the newspapers and kept abreast of political issues: the strikes in the gold mines, the behaviour of the police – who would go hunting the streets for blacks without 'passes' – and the agitation to revise the electoral laws and strike off the rolls that tiny minority of 'non-Europeans' who still retained the right to vote. (One per cent of the electorate.)

Spokesmen for the government of Generals Smuts and Herzog declared that a shared vote would lead directly to shared beds and bastardisation.

Demitrios allowed himself to be taken by some acquaintances to meetings held by the Communist Party, a noisy but ineffective little *groupuscule*. Films from the Soviet Union were shown in one of the city's cinemas. Small private gatherings were also addressed by the party's intellectuals. What he saw and heard during these meetings he guilelessly tried to pass on to the clients of the restaurants he worked in. Perhaps more provocatively still, he occasionally distributed pamphlets on behalf of the party.

It is not known who finally gave his name to police headquarters in Marshall Square. Perhaps he had also unwisely drawn attention to himself by trying to get his situation in the country regularised. In the winter he was picked up and deported forthwith to Mozambique.

From then on he was kept under surveillance by the authorities in both Mozambique and the Union of South Africa. Nor was the stigma of his mother's origins forgotten. Besides, he was incapable of holding his tongue. In Lourenço Marques he attempted to enlist in the Portuguese army, but on principle the recruiting office turned away people of mixed racial origin. Subsequently he went back to his old job of selling books and periodicals in the Akropolis department store. Within a few weeks his incessant chatter had turned his colleagues against him. He was put out in the street.

A time of great anxiety followed. His deportation from South Africa had reawakened old insecurities. He slept badly. He suffered from severe indigestion. In the early mornings he would wake to a turbulence in his stomach.

He lived in hand-to-mouth fashion, sometimes working as a porter in the docks, sometimes hanging about the Catholic mission or the Anglican church. (Many members of the Greek community used to attend divine service in the latter.) He relaxed in the company of blacks, among whom he could even play the hero, or the boss, like his father. But the more he felt himself to be going downhill socially, the less he could understand or control what he was becoming.

To his own surprise he was given a job, in the winter of 1937, by the British state airline, Imperial Airways. A new airport was being built in the most northerly province of Mozambique, on the marshy, malarial coast near Quelimane, and the firm needed a translator in Portuguese and Shangaan – though he had to struggle to master that latter language. Out in the swamps and bushveld no one cared what exactly his status was or who his antecedents had been. He could make his own way there. He learned to drive a car and chauffered his superiors around.

His leisure hours he spent studying the few technical books he could get hold of in that isolated corner of the world. Sometimes he browsed in an English translation of the Bible that the previous occupant of his quarters had left behind. During this period he made friends with a mechanical engineer from Scotland who went by the name of 'Scotty'. The man was an extrovert and a reprobate who was not much interested in Mimis's tales. He organised hunting parties that went out into the marshes not far from the mouth of the Zambesi. Plenty of game was to be found there. The employees of Imperial Airways earned pocket money by exporting buffalo meat to Rhodesia and Nyasaland.

Scotty lived with a black woman from a neighbouring tribe.

'How can you go with someone like that?' Mimis once asked.

She was terrific in bed, Scotty answered. He laughed loudly. 'She can take the skin off your dick.'

Mimis said to himself: 'Never mind.'

Alone at night in his little room, he would fantasise about his fate. His real mother must have been an exceptional woman. Just as black and no less fierce than Scotty's friend. What had actually happened between her and Michaelis? Could it be that she had brought into being some kind of new, separate tribe? Where that particular idea had come from he did not know. Perhaps she had not died, but had left his father for her own reasons, and somewhere, in a secret corner of Africa, was ruling over a group of rebellious women of mixed race. Sometimes these thoughts took forms more grotesque still. His own imaginings pursued him. They were out of control.

'Out of control,' he said in matter-of-fact fashion to Scotty. The words remained without concrete meaning, like the isolated clouds constantly moving over the head of the surprised Scotsman, travelling towards the tangled, indolent, encircling bush, and then vanishing.

Overcome by severe stomach pains, Demitrios was admitted into the nearest clinic, where his appendix was removed by a local doctor. The anaesthetic seemed to remain in his system and continued to affect his daydreams for weeks afterwards. He fell silent; stood motionless for minutes on end, unable to utter a sound; moved tentatively, like a partially sighted person. The operation seemed to him to have cut him off from his own being. His body had become what the locals called *dungeka*: obscure, husk-like, set apart.

Scotty could no longer understand him and Demitrios could hardly explain to him how he felt. In the evening, as he was about to enter his cabin, he would hear through the half-open door the cry of a muezzin, becoming one with a sound that came from the stars. At other times he heard the hissing of a snake. He would find himself in an underground vault and would be compelled to stand and listen to the snake. It made a horrible, urgent, muddy, incomprehensible sound.

These anxiety attacks went on for three or four weeks. He was hardly able to keep himself going. Such things were not uncommon in Quelimane, among both the half-crazy expatriates and the mocking, malignant indigenes. After about a month the feeling that he was under constant threat began to recede slowly. Mimis was able at last to speculate about other things. Like travel. Air travel especially. Though he had yet to set foot in an aeroplane, the idea of it roused his enthusiasm.

In January 1938 – his Quelimane experience now well behind him – he went to the South African consulate in Lourenço Marques and made yet another request for permission to enter the country. On this occasion he made sure that the translation of the Portuguese birth certificate presented to the consul showed Marika (who was registered as 'white' in the records) and not Amelia Williams as his natural mother. This manoeuvre did not help him. In July he applied to the consulate for a tourist visa merely. That too was denied him. Not even as a tourist was he welcome in South Africa. He again managed to get into the country, nevertheless.

He was determined that this time no one would know where he was going or what he was doing.

Then – silence. More than a year was to elapse before his name once again surfaces in the official South African files. This time it is because he has meticulously gone to register himself at police headquarters in Marshall Square, Johannesburg. For the following three months he attends the Progress College in the same city. He studies electrical welding, metal-cutting with an oxy-acetylene burner and how to work at a lathe. The moment he is given his certificate by the college he signs on as a member of a trade union, the Boiler Makers and Welders Union.

These are feverish times. The South African economy is expanding rapidly; the Second World War is about to break out and skilled labour is in short supply. At the beginning of May he finds work with the British Mining Supply Company in Faraday Street. The firm has recently switched to the production of armoured vehicles; his speciality becomes the production of filters and pump-cowlings.

Demitrios invests in a tailor-made suit and crocodile-leather shoes. His work turns out to be not too arduous. Whenever he doesn't want to work, or when he feels too weak to do so, he stays in bed. No one is going to make a fuss about it. He soon gets in touch with the Communists once more. He pays his monthly sub-scription of two shillings and sixpence to the party and goes up and down Loveday Street distributing leaflets. Every now and then he attends meetings on the City Hall steps or in various commu-nity centres. What he most enjoys, however, is his visits to the local library. He spends hours there, bent over the latest technical

and scientific journals. He is now interested in technology, maritime architecture, astronomy and metallurgy.

These journals make him long for 'overseas', those lands where
everything is more modern, moves more rapidly and is less provin-
cial than in South Africa. Would it not be a great thing to stand
one day in London's famous Trafalgar Square? Or among the sky-
scrapers of New York?

Twenty months after he had formally registered his presence in the
country, some anonymous official in some department or another
scrutinised the Tsafendas dossier and found that not everything in
it was as it should be. He had committed an offence under the
Aliens Act, which governed immigration in all its aspects. On 6
August 1940 he was summoned to appear before a judge. He was
found guilty of contravening the Act and sentenced either to pay
a fine of twelve pounds and ten shillings or to spend a month in
prison. Demitrios was relieved. His employers, British Mining, had
presented to the court a statement from which nothing suspicious
or untoward about him could be elicited. It had been decided that
he was not to be expelled from the country. He paid the fine
immediately and temporary papers were issued to him, on the
grounds of his claim that he was performing 'essential war service'.

But another zealous pen-licker in the Department of
Immigration and Asiatic Affairs was not satisfied. He wanted to
know why the case of Tsafendas had been dealt with so leniently –
not according to the book. This official's head of department was
persuaded to send a note to the Commissioner of Police informing
him of the following damaging facts: the man was a half-caste, a
Coloured; and a Communist too. Further: 'The above is passed to

you in order that the activities of Tsafandakis [*sic*] may be watched, and I shall be glad if you will advise me in due course should anything to his detriment become known.'

Was it for this reason that six months later Demitrios left his 'war job' with the British Mining Company? At the beginning of 1942 he applied at the consulate in Johannesburg for a Portuguese passport. The document issued to him was valid for one year only. The Greek consulate, to which he had also applied for a passport, issued him with a document which, like the other, was valid for just a single year. He knew that he would not be left to himself for much longer; the security services were watching his comings and goings. In May he left for Cape Town. His intention was to sign on with a ship sailing for Great Britain or the United States. The Greek consul in Cape Town helped him to get a berth on the cargo ship *Eugenie Livanos*. Its destination was the east coast of Canada.

On the day of his departure Mimis climbed up Table Mountain. The view over South Africa's mother-city and the bay was spectacular. To the left were the white horses of the Atlantic Ocean. To the right, in the distance, he could see the mother-of-pearl peaks of the Hottentots Holland mountains. The wind hissed among the rocks and slopes around him; the noise of the city below was barely audible. It was as if he looked at it all through a tinted wall of glass.

Many jumbled thoughts passed through his mind. He was leaving the regions of his birth in order to prove to himself that he was a man at home in the wide world; that he was no bastard but a cosmopolitan. After a while he broke off the tapering silver leaf of a shrub – which he could not name – and put it inside his pocket Bible. Then he wandered slowly down to the docks.

It is hard for us today to imagine the expectations that Cape Town harbour once aroused in the breasts of all who passed through it, whether arriving at the quasi-mythical foot of Africa, or departing from it certain of one thing only: the difficulty, perhaps the impossibility, of ever returning. The vacancy between two landfalls, the void that the ocean used to represent to those crossing it, its tedium and formlessness which engendered a longing for the shore, for any shore – all that has been lost. On a map the difference between the Cape and the 'real world' once amounted to seven thousand nautical miles; at sea it was experienced as an apparently interminable period of suspension, a yawning hiatus in the lives of all who were on board.

On 12 June 1942 Demitrios Tsafendas sailed northwards, not knowing that twenty years were to pass before he would return to the city.

The twenty-four-year-old Demitrios did not think of the ship's company of the *Eugenie Livanos* as a group of strangers. They were Greeks; they spoke his father's language; he felt that he knew their ways. But after some time he took against the hothouse atmosphere of the boat, the mutual dependence of the sailors on one another, the isolated, hierarchical nature of their closely knit society. In it he occupied the lowliest rank of all. He had the title of 'mess boy' and served the others: kneading dough in the kitchen, pulling loaves out of the oven. At first he was teased by being sent about the ship on long, pointless errands. When he complained to the officers they shrugged their shoulders and laughed.

He was on board because he had wanted to get out of South Africa. Now he found himself among rejects – some of them flamboyant, dope-smoking, foul-mouthed brandishers of knives. The ship was ruled by the ethos of 'setting the guts alight', as the Greek song put it; of the rover's existence that rotted the bowels. And it was wartime. The further north they sailed the more his unease grew. Panic overtook him when he realised that his flight might be doomed at its outset. Once they had crossed the equator, and the *Eugenie Livanos* entered the war zone of the North Atlantic – where German U-boats roamed – Demitrios withdrew into himself and fell sick. He pined for landfall long before they finally entered Canadian waters.

No sooner had the boat berthed in St John's harbour than he packed his few things together and fled.

It was autumn in America. He was picked up by the police near Montreal. He begged the Canadian authorities not to send him back to the *Livanos*. He spent months under informal arrest in Halifax, Nova Scotia. The Canadians were not sure what to do with him.

In the winter of 1942 he escaped, together with two other sailors who had jumped ship. After a journey of five hundred kilometres they reached the border of the United States. On foot and in daunting conditions Demitrios crossed the frozen St Croix River. Three weeks later he was picked up in Bangor, Maine, and arrested for entering the United States illegally. On his arrest he started babbling nonsense, gibberish; with some deliberateness, in all likelihood, he presented himself to his captors as a man who was deeply disturbed. These were the circumstances of his first admission to a psychiatric institution. It was attached to a hospital in Boston. He did his best there to convince the doctors that he heard voices, that horrible voices spoke to him out of the hospital's central heating system. After a while he no longer needed to exaggerate the state he was in; it seemed that the long ocean voyage had indeed unhinged him.

Any hope of getting permission to reside in the United States, which had been his original aim, was now ruled out. Demitrios's next four years were spent either in detention or in service on the so-called 'Liberty Ships' – cheaply and hastily built freighters which sailed the Atlantic in convoys to supply the Allies with food and arms. He was taken six times altogether into different institutions during this period, sometimes in a serious condition, sometimes with complaints that appear to have been trifling, even to one who knows what was to become of him subsequently. Each time he was discharged he was sent straight back to sea. When he was not in hospital he was on board ship – always against his will.

The spring of 1945 found him on another Greek vessel, the *Marina Nicolao*. From there he wrote a letter to President Roosevelt complaining that over the last few years he had spent no more than twenty-nine days ashore and at liberty. Now that Nazi Germany was on the point of capitulating, could his 'war service' not be taken into account, and permission for him to reside legally in the United States finally be granted?

From March 1946 onwards he spent eighteen months on land, in the North Grafton State Hospital, Massachusetts. The prognosis, according to the doctors, was poor. Demitrios hallucinated: he dreamed of a girl who was waiting for him somewhere in southern Africa, but at the same time he was fatally convinced that all his progeny would be black. In January 1947 his condition was described as 'hebephrenic schizophrenia'. Hebephrenia is another term for congenital retardation. Six months later he was declared cured and discharged. The doctors wanted him to be repatriated, and in the meantime details of his previous life had filtered through to the authorities. The fact that he had been a member of the Communist Party was regarded as even more sinister in postwar America than it had been in the Transvaal some years earlier.

The officials who knitted their brows over Demitrios's future had to determine who he was and to what country he belonged. No simple answer could be expected to either question, for they were dealing with someone who had as many names as personalities.

Was he the illegitimate son of a lathe-operator now living in Pretoria? A Mozambican agitator? A South African *métique* with a Greek background? A deranged sailor? 'Retarded' he plainly was not. Apart from fluent Greek, English and Portuguese, he spoke Shangaan, Arabic and a little Afrikaans. His Greek and Portuguese passports had long since expired. He possessed the papers of an American seaman, but these were of doubtful value. South Africa offered no solution to the problem: only a clear indication that he would not be welcome there. The authorities confirmed that they had refused him a visa several times already and would do so again if he should seek one.

Somewhere in those offices, with their bakelite telephones and packed filing cabinets, the knot was finally severed. Demitrios Tsafandakis, it was declared, was *definitely* Greek.

In August a deportation order was issued. A month later, under police escort, he was put aboard the S.S. *Marine Jumbo*. The ship was about to sail to the Mediterranean and to call at Piraeus, the port for the city of Athens.

Piraeus in the sunset light of 1947. The harbour a random assemblage of fortified, bomb-battered structures. Hawkers and barrows swarming on the pavements. The 'Kafenia' filled with men, men only, most of them moustached and unemployed. The daily papers under strict censorship. Streets reeking of petrol and sesame. Turkish hubble-bubbles for hire. On every corner rousing gramophone music of the kind Demitrios can remember from his parents' house in Lourenço Marques. He is at last free, ashore legally, done with the fear of being followed.

Not that all was well. A civil war was in progress. German occupation and years of starvation had been succeeded by guerilla fighting; now an outright war was being fought between the Left and the Right. Demitrios had arrived in a country with an empty stomach and darkness at its heart. Yet he was about to enjoy a period that was free of the attacks that had been tormenting him since leaving Cape Town. It was as if here, precisely here, he had at last acquired some of the stoic fatalism which the Greeks think of as peculiarly their own. Like many another macho Greek, he also learned to boast and complain. He talked himself into a job with the American Reconstruction Mission, a sub-section of the Marshall Plan. He worked first as a translator, subsequently in the section dealing with the delivery of supplies to American and British troops. He had status again, he used his languages, he bought a hat.

Nevertheless he applied more than once for a visa to reside in South Africa, or at least to visit the country, and in the letters accompanying these applications he did his best to deny that he actually 'belonged' to Europe. A hectoring tone began to enter into his correspondence with both the South African Department of External Affairs and the American authorities. 'I was sent to Greece, a country I have never seen before . . . It is not a small mistake. The difference is between the North Pole and the South Pole.' He insisted that South Africa was the country in which he had been educated and that it was 'the country of my mother, Amelia Williams'. Just as he had done previously in the United States, he told the story about the woman who had remained faithful to him for so long. 'Will you please permit me to go home again, and to return to the girl with whom I grew up, whom I want to marry, and with whom I have so much in common.' And in conclusion: 'I am here a man without a country . . . I have a lot more to mention but cannot put it into writing.'

This letter ends with the words, 'Remain Yours, James Demitrios Tsafandakis.'

He had acquired the name James in Piraeus. In all likelihood this was the consequence of his having become a member of a group of young men and women who kept in touch with what they called, simply enough, The Christian Church. They used occasionally to meet in one of the suburbs of Athens in order to study the Scriptures. The chief language of the group was English. It was not exactly a church; nor was it a sect or cult; rather a vague, pleasant fellowship of faith with world-wide contacts. Its doctrines, so far as there were any, emphasised the equality of all races, a not very strictly observed abstinence from alcohol, and a peace-loving, almost American kind of optimism. His conversion to the faith had been confirmed by baptism in the sea, along with his new name. Shortly after his dismissal from the Reconstruction Mission, the thirty-year-old but already corpulent James, wearing only his underpants, had been ritually immersed in the waves near Piraeus. After the ceremony he was joyfully applauded and thrown on to the sandy beach.

He lived in Greece for almost two years – that is, for about as long a period as he had spent on the Witwatersrand. Then restlessness and chronic anxiety struck at him again. In the late summer of 1949 he worked for some time on a Greek cruise-ship, the *Corinthia*, which went from port to port around the Mediterranean. In Marseilles he left the ship and travelled to Paris, where he applied for a visa to Spain. On 8 November he arrived at a Portuguese border post, Barca d'Alva, only to be arrested by the guards on duty.

He spent a month under arrest in Oporto, while the Policia Internaçional e de Defesa do Estado (President Salazar's notorious secret police) examined his baptismal certificate. The refugee passport given to him in Athens revealed that he had been deported several times from the United States. His putative Portuguese citizenship was investigated and confirmed from Lourenço Marques. But in that case why had he never been called up for military service? Immediately he was declared to be a deserter and locked up. Three months later he appeared before a military tribunal in Lisbon. The PIDE reported that the Mozambique administrators had described him as an unwanted person of alien descent who would not be permitted to re-enter the province. The PIDE report also acknowledged, however, that he was not wholly accountable for his own actions. He was a rogue *que tem una vida sempre instável e de aventuras* – 'constantly drawn to an unstable and adventurous way of life'.

The rogue was set free, given temporary papers, and allowed to remain in Portugal.

From there he wrote letters to his family in Pretoria. They did not respond. They had no intention of helping him; such feelings of affection as they might once have had were now dead.

For the next year or so he could be seen wandering about the banks of the Tagus, earning his keep by hawking assorted goods of the cheapest kind: little combs, sunglasses, plastic whirligigs. He liked to go aboard ships in the harbour and gossip with their crews. He also made himself as agreeable as he could around the offices of the Companhia Naçional de Navigaçâo. Through his connections there he eventually succeeded in getting a job at sea once more. Destination: Mozambique.

October 1951: the cargo vessel S.S. *Save* makes its way through the Straits of Gibraltar, sails east and passes along the Suez Canal. Within a couple of weeks the coasts of East Africa have been left behind. Now it enters Delagoa Bay and is moored in the harbour of Lourenço Marques. Demitrios leans over the railing. What he sees is too beautiful to be believed: the busy quay, and, beyond the warehouses, the city of his birth.

Once ashore, however, he is held by passport control. 'Dimitrie Tsafandakis' is known to them as a Communist, a draft-dodger, a troublemaker. His papers may be in order but he is not allowed to proceed further. He puts up a protest against this treatment, before returning unwillingly to his ship. At noon he reports to its sickbay, doubled over with stomach pains, barely able to keep on his feet. He appears to be suffering from an acute attack of appendicitis. A decision is taken to admit him urgently to a hospital in the city.

No sooner is he off the ship than his condition improves remarkably. He has no time to lose. An hour or two later he sneaks out of the hospital and makes his way to the honorary Greek consul. He needs a Greek passport to enable him to travel from Lourenço Marques to Pretoria. Surely that is little enough to request?

The consul for Greece was Tony Maw – that same Tony Maw who had been a neighbour of Michaelis Tsafandakis many years before, in the Rua Andrade Corvo. He remembered Mimis both as the little half-breed who had been sent to his grandmother in Alexandria and as a schoolboy. Now he was back in his office, after all this time, not lost forever in the wilderness of the world: a strong, sun-tanned, loutish fellow, beefy but well-spoken, complaining about his treatment at the hands of the Portuguese.

For his part Demitrios was confident that he had come to the right place. He was dealing with a friend of his father's, after all. He hadn't seen his family for ten years, he said; he had been blocked and frustrated everywhere, and especially so by the PIDE and the South Africans. It was more than time that he visited Michaelis, who was now sixty-six years old and was waiting impatiently to see his long-lost, first-born son.

Maw was not inclined to oblige this interloper by issuing him with a travel document, though it would have been little enough trouble for him to do it. Demitrios had arrived in the office out of the blue. He was not even a Greek citizen, formally speaking.

His father was indeed known to Maw, but it now transpired that Tsafandakis had never taken the trouble to register the birth of his illegitimate child with the consulate. Let him plead as much as he liked; the consul was determined to stick to the letter of the law. All else aside, Demitrios had feigned illness in order to get ashore. He was an illegal immigrant. What could he have been thinking of? Nothing could be simpler, the Englishman said threateningly, than for him to phone the police. He'd be deported immediately.

'Do you know anything about my natural mother?' Demitrios asked, more in an attempt to distract Maw than in hope of rousing his compassion. 'I spent years looking for her grave. To tell the truth I'm not even sure that she is actually dead.'

The consul was not impressed. He had never known Amelia, he said curtly. According to report she was not someone who was fit to have been a lifetime's companion for the goodhearted Michaelis. She was black, 'a native'.

Demitrios hesitantly took his hat off his head. His legs began to tremble. He did not know what to say. A few minutes later Maw told the eccentric seaman to clear off.

'Just remember that one day I won't want a Greek Orthodox funeral,' Demitrios shouted weakly, from outside the office.

Not long after this episode the authorities returned him to Lisbon. He was trapped like an eel in a basket, it seemed, and would never escape. His old ailments duly reappeared. In the Hospital do Ultramar a diagnosis was made: '*parasitose intestinal; psicose maníaco-depressiva*'. However, on this occasion the parasites in his intestines and brain apparently responded rapidly to treatment, for he was discharged from the hospital after a mere three weeks.

The PIDE was convinced that he was up to no good. He was arrested trying to cross the border into Spain; for this he spent the next eleven months in jail. Initially he was kept in the 'Aljube', where political prisoners were interrogated; later in one of the cells in Fort Calxias. In both places he was manhandled as never before. Nothing in his previous experience had prepared him for it. A couple of times he feared for his life. No cock would have crowed if he had been put up against a wall: in the Portugal of the dictator Salazar anything was possible. But the interrogations yielded nothing and towards the end of April 1953 he was set free.

He found himself in the Albergue de Mendicidade de Mitra, a shelter for the homeless which was run by an order of mendicant friars in Lisbon. He became a pedlar once again. Along the quays and avenues of the capital he carried his wares: lacework, this time, and local embroidery, along with various other gewgaws.

The extent and complexity of Tsafendas's wanderings stun the imagination. But it is possible to discern one common theme running through them. During the two decades he spent outside South Africa the sea was the only constant presence in his life. He remained almost exclusively on the coastline of the countries he lived in, in cities where the docks beckoned him and where the sounds of winches, seagulls and motors rose above the hiss and roar of the ocean. Piraeus, Oporto, Lisbon, Marseilles, London, Hamburg – he was most himself amid the restless, provisional lives of people who did not know where they might be the next day or the day after it. It was as if an unspoken judgement had been passed on him, once he had reached a certain age and had gone a certain distance: he had to serve out his days within earshot of the sombre clamour of waves and spray.

In all likelihood Demitrios would never have managed to get back to South Africa, had it not been for the profound unpredictability of circumstance that was organic to his way of life. In the nineteen fifties and the early sixties it appeared he would never succeed in returning to the subcontinent. And one may wonder why he longed to return there, where he would be more conspicuous than anywhere else, and above all where he would be regarded as a half-man, a member of a sub-species. From 1951 onwards his name appears on the official list of those banned from entering South Africa – the so-called blacklist. In Portugal the PIDE would always be suspicious of him. From the United States he had been permanently excluded. A period in Germany had ended in the Ochsenzoll Clinic; after his discharge from that institution he was despatched to Lisbon, where he again plied his trade as a hawker along the Tagus and in the city's parks. Some two years later he attended the Brussels trade fair, optimistically bringing with him a stock of Portuguese embroidery. For the failure of this particular venture he later blamed 'the Chinese competition'. In the spring of 1959, after a further spell in Germany, he decided (in his own words) 'to leave western Europe and try my luck in England'.

The move did nothing to change his luck. As a foreigner, the holder of a Portuguese passport, he was denied an official work permit. Casual jobs were hard to come by, and he found the place and the people unfriendly. Nevertheless he managed to keep himself going until the autumn. Always a lover of public debate, he was fascinated by Speakers' Corner in Hyde Park and went to meetings of the Labour Party at Caxton Hall, where he listened to speeches by Barbara Castle and the future Prime Minister, James Callaghan. He also attended gatherings of the nascent anti-apartheid movement, and, more unexpectedly, established contact with a self-styled 'Neo-Labour' group which used the North Middlesex Cricket Club – of all improbable venues – as its meeting place. There were a number of disaffected, anti-apartheid ex-South Africans in this group, one of whom remembered 'Tsafandakis' explicitly introducing himself to them as a Cape Coloured. He was eager, he said, 'to create resistance to the regime', though he had no plausible suggestions to make about how this might be done. While in London he made a further attempt to gain entry papers for South Africa; that approach, like all those which had preceded it, was firmly rebuffed by the authorities.

Early in his stay in London he was admitted for examination to both University College Hospital and the Hospital for Tropical Diseases; each time he came in complaining of stomach disorders. Predictably enough the doctors were unable to help him. He did not blame them for their failure; to him it was evidence of how difficult and special his case was. Later his condition deteriorated radically. In mid-September he was admitted to the St Pancras Hospital in a psychotic state. The episode was a brief one; but it was followed by a more protracted collapse which led to a two months' confinement in the Whitecroft Hospital on the Isle of Wight. On his release the authorities gave him a choice: he could be sent back either to Germany or to Portugal. Staying on in the

United Kingdom was out of the question. Demitrios chose Germany. From there he made yet another attempt to reach southern Africa.

Overland, this time.

On 30 June 1960 Demitrios left by train from Munich for the Balkans. After a short stop in Piraeus he travelled to Alexandria, the city of his childhood. Arriving there in October, he was arrested almost immediately. Towards the end of that year he was helped by the Red Cross to get a passage on a boat going to Beirut. Some weeks later his presence in East Jerusalem was noted. He made an effort to enter Israel, carrying a small suitcase in each hand. He was absolutely penniless and he could not convince the officials at the Mandelbaum Gate of his good intentions. 'Is there no place here for a mendicant monk?' he demanded of them. An investigator was summoned and after a short conversation he was sent back to the Jordanian sector of the city. A note was taken of the interview and thus Tsafendas's name was entered into the dossiers of the Mossad too.

For months Mimis went back and forth across the two sides of the Jordan River. The little Arabic he spoke, so far from helping him, was a source of unease to the people he encountered and on at least one occasion led to an ugly misunderstanding. This was when he had to be treated by a Jerusalem doctor – Dr Theodore Phylactopoulos – for a broken nose. Claiming to be a political refugee, he also visited the Spanish embassy in East Jerusalem. But the Spaniards were not prepared to help him get a visa to Israel. Finally he left Jordan on a bus which was bound for Beirut via Damascus.

He was unable to find work in Lebanon. He set out once more by bus, this time heading towards Tripoli, and subsequently to Aleppo, in Syria. From Aleppo it was possible to reach Adana, in Turkey. A difficult trek through the snow-covered passes of the Toros mountains brought him to Ankara. Demitrios – the Wandering Greek – had in the meantime grown a beard. His upper jaw was inflamed. His teeth were in a bad state, some of them had crumbled away, and he suffered constantly from pain in his gums.

After a month in Ankara he had picked up some Turkish, a language which his father had been able to speak. There were several things here which reminded him of Michaelis: Turkish cuisine, the songs he heard in the tea houses. Even the physical appearance of the men, and a certain pride or boldness in their gaze, as well as their habit of sharing the pleasures of a hubble-bubble pipe on the pavement, seemed reminiscent to him, like a vague echo of the lives of the Cretan forebears he had never known. The same was true of Istanbul. The look of the streets struck him as somehow familiar too, and he himself went about unnoticed through them. With his beard and his belly he could easily be taken for any down-and-out Muslim.

For want of anything better he sold his blood regularly to the Istanbul blood transfusion service. Most of the money he earned in this way – for each pint he was paid about an average week's wage in Turkey – he spent on the dentist. His upper teeth were ground, the incisors filed down, and a gold bridge fitted. Over it was spread a silver layer. At the age of thirty-five Demitrios had acquired a steely smile.

Later he got a job in the Tarhaban College. He taught English, and for a while lived with a Turkish woman working in the same institution as himself. She did what she could for him, and with a word here and a word there managed to get a residence permit for him. In winter the relationship between them deteriorated; when he left the city – this time for Lisbon via Rome – he carried in his wallet a reference from the college. In it he was described as a teacher of English phonetics.

After seaman, translator, lathe-operator, hawker and pilgrim, he now described himself, when the opportunity arose, as 'Professor of English'.

Then the unexpected happened. For the first time Marika answered one of his letters. A full year after the event he learned that his father had died. Mimis wrote back to Marika to let her know that he was still unable to get a visa to enter South Africa, but nevertheless he expected to receive his share of the inheritance. By this time he was back in Lisbon. Soon after receiving her letter he went to the South African embassy and applied for a visa. The young woman at the desk told him in a loud voice that the request was pointless. He had been blacklisted by the Ministry of External Affairs, and instead of wasting his money in trying to get a visa he would do better to spend it on something useful. A clean shirt, for instance. Demitrios fell into a rage. He tore up the application form he had been completing and threw the scraps into her face. Then, still enraged, he left the building.

His next stop was the shelter for the homeless run by the mendicant friars of Mitra, in which he had taken refuge once before. But he soon got on the wrong side of his benefactors there. They said he made trouble among the other inmates. They were tired of listening to his lectures about Palestine, the Bible, and the bad state of affairs in Portugal's colonies. The friars wrote letters to Pretoria: could the man's family not take care of him? He was lonely and longed for a home. They even got in touch with the PIDE. Why could Demitrios not go back to the country of his birth? He was now forty-five; the whole issue of his conscription had in effect been resolved by the passage of time.

It is hard to know who, if anyone, might have been pulling the strings behind the scenes. In August 1963 Demitrios heard that the colonial administration of Mozambique, after thirteen years of hostility, had granted him a sort of amnesty. The brothers of the Albergue de Mendicidade de Mitra paid for his passage on a ship called the *Principi Perfecto*.

Early in October the *Principi Perfecto* steamed into Delagoa Bay. Once ashore in Lourenço Marques, Demitrios went to stay with his aunt Anna, Marika's sister, who in earlier years had occasionally protected him against the wrath of the family. At Anna's request Marika arrived from Pretoria a few days later. She told him straight out that Michaelis had left nothing to his oldest son. The family had never been well-off: that was something he must understand once and for all. The little properties Michaelis had owned he had left to his daughters, as their dowry. There had never been anything else.

He was deeply disappointed. Could she, he asked, at least arrange for him to stay under her roof in the Transvaal? For a while? Marika phoned her brother in Pretoria. He owned a motor car. It was agreed that Victor would come and fetch them.

On Saturday morning, 2 November, Demitrios went to the

South African consulate in Lourenço Marques and asked for a permit that would allow him a period of temporary residence in the Republic of South Africa. A Mr J. van der Berg, the official responsible, made a cursory search for the name of Tsafendas on the 'Stop List', and failed to find it. As far as J. van der Berg was concerned, the man was in possession of a valid Portuguese passport, in which he was described as resident in Mozambique. He was accompanied by members of a family with South African identity papers. Besides, van der Berg was sure that had there been anything suspect about this Tsafendas, he would certainly have heard of it from the PIDE.

On Monday 4 November, the family – Demitrios, Marika, Victor and Anna – passed into South Africa via the customs post at Komatipoort.

The South Africa that Demitrios was entering was in most respects the same country as the one he had left two decades before – only worse. The Afrikaner Nationalist Party, under Verwoerd, was still in the saddle and ruling as relentlessly as ever. Segregation was enforced even more strictly than before: laws against mixed marriages and sexual acts between the different races were in effect, as were draconian pass laws ('movement control' was their stated aim). Forcible clearances of black and mixed-race areas in larger and smaller cities took place on a regular basis. After the Sharpeville rebellion of 1960 the Prime Minister had adumbrated an ideology of so-called 'separate development', which involved the delineation of Bantustans for the blacks. The resounding logic of the programme – white tribalism fortified, deepened, aggrandised – astonished even his own supporters. In practice it meant little more than large-scale deportations of blacks to various remote, impoverished corners of the country.

Mimis stepped eagerly into his brother's house. As far as he was concerned he had come home an older and wiser person. He bought a bicycle.

5   AFRICA AGAIN

W<small>HY WAS</small> D<small>EMITRIOS</small> never regarded as a hero by the black population of South Africa? Admittedly, after the assassination in
1966 his name was used by some black youths as a kind of
byword. 'I'll Tsafendas you' meant 'I'll cut you up for good and
always.' Anyone who could stab a man three or four times in a
matter of seconds, while virtually every member of parliament
looked on, had to be thought of as a master craftsman, a specialist. So plainly did this appear to be the case that rumours began to
go around that Demitrios had been professionally trained. The
persistence of these rumours eventually compelled the doctors
who conducted the autopsy to conclude their report with the

words, 'The wounds were not inflicted by an expert, but were in fact perfectly ordinary* for such an attack.'

It did not take long, after his return to Pretoria in 1963, for things to go badly between Mimis and his family. Initially he boarded with his half-brother Victor. After just a few days Victor had had enough of this arrangement. Demitrios was an eccentric, restless, troubling person to have in the house. He got up at five a.m. and stood next to his bed with his Bible open in his hand. He was convinced that his travels abroad had given him a wisdom that the provincials around him lacked. He would give instructions to anyone he came across and made a habit of interfering in other people's business. That, at any rate, was his half-brother's view of him.

His stepmother and half-sister Evangelina also found him a handful. He would hold forth to them about his travels and about The Christian Church, with whose members in the Transvaal he had managed to make contact. It was difficult to get any sense out of much of what he said. Marika regretted bringing him back with her from Lourenço Marques. He could not accept the fact that he had not come into an inheritance of any kind. At meals he stuffed himself shamelessly. Marika's grandchildren laughed at the way he ate. They thought of him as a kind of hippopotamus, a hippo who carried them about on his back, barked like a dog, and sometimes rode on his bike with them in the city parks. He was a remarkable sight on his bicycle. People stared after him. He was oversized and wore a stetson hat.

* With a peculiar insensitivity, the authors of the report used at this point the Afrikaans word *doodgewoon* – i.e. 'dead ordinary'.

A week after his arrival he was caught going through Marika's desks and cupboards in search of his father's effects. Marika and Victor gave him some money and told him to be on his way.

For the next six months Demitrios worked as a welder and an odd-job man in Pretoria. He paid regular visits to his brother-in-law, Nikos Vlachopoulos, who, with Demitrios's half-sister, Helena, managed the Proclamation Hill Cafe. He would spend hours there, reading the newspapers and receiving acquaintances as if he was holding audience with them. At the beginning of July his current employers, F.A. Poole (Pty.) Ltd., moved from Carl Street to an industrial area outside Pretoria. This move involved a stocktaking, in the course of which Demitrios fell out with the foreman. Some days later he was fired. That same day he applied to the Department of External Affairs for an exit visa.

Demitrios felt optimistic about his future. His papers were in order, he could go where he liked, he could even think of himself as a kind of tourist in southern Africa. In July 1964 he crossed the border into Rhodesia. He had fifty pounds in his pocket. In Marandellas, near Salisbury, he visited his sister Katerina, now Mrs Pnevma. Her husband was unpleasantly surprised by the arrival of this new-found half-brother, whom Katerina barely remembered: a man who had been rejected by the family and who brought with him an unpleasant reputation. An hour's conversation between them was enough. Demitrios was told to move on.

So he went to Nyasaland. From the capital, Blantyre, he travelled to Lake Nyasa in the company of a fish-trader. Failing to find work there he returned to Salisbury. At the end of August the

British South Africa Police deported him on the grounds that his entry permit had expired. He used his Portuguese passport to return to Mozambique. The end of the year found him living in the town of Gondola and working for the Hume Pipelaying Company.

At weekends he would drink a few glasses of beer with members of the local Greek community. They were impressed by his travels and his command of languages, but they also thought that he talked a lot of nonsense, especially about Portugal's colonies. Sometimes he declaimed biblical texts at them. An Orthodox priest who visited Gondola from Umtali, in Rhodesia, spread the rumour that he was actually not a Greek but a Turk.

On one occasion he admitted to people he met at an hotel in Gondola that he was the black sheep of his family. When they appeared not to understand him, Demitrios took off his hat and showed them the greying, tight-packed curls of his hair. 'That's why they won't have me near them,' he said. He declared that one day a complete mingling of the races would finally take place in Africa. Everyone then would be a bastard. They would all come together in bed; and God would find it good.

One member of his audience angrily banged his glass down on the table; the others burst out laughing.

On another occasion Demitrios was standing at the bar with a group of black employees of the Hume Company. He was in high spirits – speaking to them in their own language and, it seemed to others present, instructing them as though they were his disciples.

'This isn't going to last long,' he shouted out suddenly, in

Portuguese. 'This country isn't called Portugal; it's called the United States of Mozambique.'

All the whites in the room pricked up their ears.

'Any day all this will come to an end. We mustn't be fooled into calling ourselves Portuguese here, because we're Africans. We'll have a blue flag. With a rainbow on it.'

In southern Africa the rainbow was (and still is) the symbol of a multi-coloured society.

'Long live our country, the United States of Mozambique!' he cried.

The following day he was picked up by agents of the PIDE. He was taken to the port of Beira, and handed over to the local commandant, Captain Luis Tavara. Subsequently he was interrogated by another officer, Inspector Horacio Ferreira.

A rainbow of races? The United States of Mozambique? How could he think of saying such things in public? This was subversive propaganda, political agitation, and worse.

So far from being cowed by these accusations, Demitrios told his interrogators that it was more than time that free elections were held in the country. He also reminded them, provocatively, that he was working on the oil pipeline, a strategic asset essential to the economy and to the survival of the whites. The Portuguese administration had a monopoly in the supply of fuel to the colony, but only the whites were profiting from it.

Ferreira was determined to find out if this troublemaker had made contact with the terrorists of Frelimo (the Mozambique Liberation Front). Demitrios was kept for ten weeks in preventive detention. He asked for some of his books to be sent over from

Pretoria, so that he would have something to read and would be able to keep in touch with the members of The Christian Church in Durban and Cape Town.

By mid-January the investigation had led nowhere. The mendicant monks had been consulted; the headquarters of the PIDE in Lisbon had also turned in a report. The conclusions drawn about him were no different from those that had been minuted in 1950, 1953 and 1962. Many years had passed since he had last been admitted into a psychiatric ward, but he was once again declared to be 'fundamentally a psychopath'. Ultimately Inspector Ferreira found the ever lengthening tale of his wanderings around the world pointless and bewildering. At the end of January he closed the dossier and let Demitrios go.

On 5 March he boarded the Indian passenger-liner, the *Karanja*. The journey from Beira to Durban took just two days. On the morning of the eighth he was admitted to the Republic of South Africa. He came ashore with two suitcases and some cooking utensils in a cardboard box. He was never to leave the country again.

He rented a room in the central area of Durban and went to look for the Cuban Hat Tearoom, near the north beach. The owner of the tearoom, Kyriakos Skordis, had been recommended to him. Skordis had no work for him, but told him he could use the place as a postal address. A few days later Demitrios called by to say that he had been registered at the local court as a translator in Greek and Portuguese. When he next visited the tearoom it was to say that he had got a job with the South African Railways. As he was obviously broke, the railways' personnel department advanced him some money and admitted him into a hostel for its employees. The work was tedious: he had to couple and uncouple the vacuum-hoses connecting one carriage to another and do minor electrical repairs. After three weeks he had had enough of it. A week later he left his depressing room in the hostel. He took from it the Gideon Bible he had found in its chest of drawers. By then he had already managed to get himself a new position. This was in the little trading town of Mandini, a hundred kilometres north of Durban. He was going to work there as a fitter for the firm of Fraser & Chalmers Ltd.

In May Demitrios was admitted to the hospital in Mandini with a severe stab wound in his left arm. He and a colleague, a fellow Greek by the name of Nikos Vergas, had had an argument in the Fraser & Chalmers canteen. In the course of it Demitrios knocked Vergas off his feet. Vergas came back at him with a knife he had drawn from his back pocket. The wound on Demitrios's arm was fourteen centimetres long. He laid a charge against his opponent and both men appeared before the local magistrate a few days later. As the quarrel between them had been conducted in Greek throughout, none of the witnesses could say what it had been about. Demitrios volunteered to act as translator, but since he was a party to the case his offer was not accepted.

Case dismissed.

'Communist bastard,' Vergas shouted after him, out in the street.

Some time after this incident Father Hanno Probst of the Roman Catholic mission to Zululand drove into Mandini. He called at the post office, as he always did, and at the local general dealers in the main street. Leaving the store, he noticed a middle-aged man sitting in the sun on a bench. His left arm was swathed in a bandage.

He was reading a newspaper. Probst was struck by his dejected expression.

The priest was from southern Germany originally. During the many years he had spent in South Africa he had acquired a sharp eye for the physical characteristics which distinguished the races from one another: subtle gradations in pigmentation and bone-structure, differences in the shape of the nose and the curls of the hair. He was proud of his refined powers of observation in this regard, especially as such indicators were considered to be of life-and-death significance in those days. To his eye the man with the injured arm was plainly a Coloured. He was convinced of it immediately. But he was sure, too, that he was not a South African.

'If you don't mind my asking, are you a Mozambican?'

The man looked up morosely.

'You're far from home, aren't you?'

'How do you know I come from there?'

'Oh, I've been around a lot. It's a hobby of mine, to guess where people come from.'

The Mozambican moved up on the bench. He too had travelled a great deal, he said. Soon he was boasting in front of the stranger. Apart from English, he said, he knew seven languages. Probst tried him in Spanish and Italian. To his surprise the man spoke both languages fairly well; his Portuguese, not surprisingly, was fluent. Then there was his German too: spoken, after some hesitation, with an unmistakable Bavarian accent. Probst was astonished. What was a man with a command of these languages up to in this remote corner of Zululand?

'You must have had very good teachers in Moscow,' the priest said suddenly, to throw the other off balance.

'And you in Rome,' the man answered after a short silence, and with an odd turn in his voice.

Hanno Probst, who was dressed in mufti, admitted that he was indeed a Roman Catholic priest, and that he lived on the mission station in the Mangete reserve, not far from a place called Mtunzini. They did a lot of good work there.

Suddenly excited, the man burst out: 'You Catholics are all the same. Profiteers. Exploiters. Look at Salazar. Those little nuns in Mozambique – you know what they do? They pump insulin into the blacks. They think there are too many of them, so they just do away with them. And the Portuguese know all about it.'

'You're a Communist,' Probst cried out.

The Communist folded up his newspaper and casually strolled towards the filling station nearby.

The meeting left Probst nonplussed. Was he indeed a *métique*, he wondered, or a European? In any case, someone ought to be warned about him. The next morning he once again drove fifty kilometres along the coast road, from his mission station to Mandini. The little town did not have a police station, so he went instead to the security office of the biggest local factory, S.A. Pulp and Paper Industries on the Tugela River. The officials there listened attentively to his story. They assured the priest they would pass the information he had given them on to the police at Nyoni. Clearly the man was dangerous. One Nikos Vergas had been in to see them not long before, bearing much the same kind of information.

Demitrios picked up his post at the Cuban Hat Tearoom towards the end of August. Among the items waiting for him was a little note from a certain Helen Daniels, a member of The Christian Church. She was a pious, single, Coloured woman from Cape Town. She wrote that she was eager to get to know him, as she had heard much about him from others. The possibility of marriage was not excluded.

That night he packed his bags once again.

In one big case he put the following: a brown suit, jerseys and a raincoat, two cream-coloured jackets, underpants, socks, four handkerchiefs and twelve neckties, a pillowslip, two green sheets, a blue blanket, two hats and various items of dirty laundry. Mixed up with these items were his books and papers, including: *Poems Old and New, The Concise Oxford English Dictionary, A Hebrew Grammar*, an *Afrikaans Exercise Book, Ogretmen not defteri* (property of the Tarhaban College, Istanbul), *An die Freunde Des Practical English, Compêndio da Gramátika Francesca, Gramática de Xisonga*, a map of Athens, the Gideon Society Bible he had taken from the railwaymen's hostel, and a medical manual about intestinal disorders and acute stomach ulcers.

The other case contained: a carpenter's square, two bolts, a tin opener, needles, eleven keys, two rolls of cotton, a saw, two combs, a pair of welder's goggles, a pair of reading glasses, a little tin containing buttons, a pair of swimming trunks, a dishcloth, hair brushes, two saucepans with lids, one saucepan without a lid, a toaster, a hammer, a file, a spirit level, two pairs of shoes, a plastic helmet, a spoon, a fork, two pairs of striped pyjamas, a little pot of glue, a mirror and a bar of soap.

He set off the next day. Having arranged a lift as far as Port Elizabeth with a commercial traveller, he loaded all his gear into the boot of a Ford sedan. From Port Elizabeth he continued his journey by rail. After a journey of two days his train halted under the elaborate Victorian iron roof of Cape Town's main railway station. He was back in the city he had left in 1942. He felt that there was something not quite right inside him. It was as if he had a slight fever. Or as if a hunger of an unfamiliar kind was gnawing at him.

6 THE MAN WITH STEEL TEETH

SOMETIMES ONE CANNOT help wishing that everything, for centuries past, had been captured on film. In technicolor. With each individual life no more than a small segment of the entire show.

Who, in such a case, would turn his gaze away from Demitrios Tsafendas, newly arrived at the main Cape Town railway station, carrying with him two suitcases containing a bundle of dirty linen and a collection of pots, pans and cutlery?

But were one truly in a position to play this game, what moments from any life would one actually choose to witness? In the context of Tsafendas's tormented career, his murderous assault in the House of Assembly – which took place exactly one year and nine days after his arrival in Cape Town – might appear, bizarrely enough, as an almost inconsequential or marginal event. Why should one choose to witness a thirty-year-old murder if one might instead hear again the long-vanished shuffle on linoleum of two pairs of shoes, in a nondescript house in the suburb of Bellville South? It was there, in the front room of the house, in the middle of the Cape winter, that Tsafendas met for the first time the woman who had indicated to him that she wished to become his wife. Her name was Helen Daniels. She was thirty-five years old. How did they greet each other? What did they say next?

Her father and brother had gone in their car to the station, where they had picked him up. Helen knew nothing about him, other than that he had travelled the world and that he was a member of the fellowship, The Christian Church, to which she and her family belonged. She had written two or three letters to him earlier in the winter, and had also sent a snapshot of herself, asking him to do the same for her. But that request had been ignored. In the end she knew only his handwriting. Demitrios wrote his letters with a fountain-pen, in a strikingly elegant, self-assured, un-South African hand. From what he had actually put down little had emerged.

When he made a flesh-and-blood appearance at the gate to the front garden, and then advanced towards the door of her parents' home, she took somewhat against him. He had a double chin. She had imagined him to be less stout in build. He was unshaven; there were holes in his jersey; and his bags – those battered suit-cases, those pots and pans – made him look like some kind of hawker carrying his goods from door to door. Still, this out-of-luck pedlar (which was what he reminded her of) had good manners.

Demitrios took a seat. He drank his tea and began to tell his tales. He had served in American warships and had once been torpedoed. He knew Europe like the palm of his hand. He had been in Palestine and visited the holy places and wandered along the banks of the Jordan. That he spilled some of his tea in his saucer, Helen felt, should not be held against him.

When her father began to pray and sing hymns, after they had drunk their tea, Demitrios joined in fervently. Obviously there was nothing amiss with his faith. He was shown the little room which had been set aside for him. It was agreed he would lodge temporarily with them in Sans Souci Street. They knew that on his identity document their lodger was registered as a white, and that they were therefore breaking the law in letting him stay under their roof.

Helen was left feeling ill-at-ease about her suitor. Her distrustful glances had not escaped him, though his stories about the Middle East, about his Greek father and his natural mother, had softened the first, rather unfavourable impression he had made on her. He had let it be understood between them that henceforth he planned to live his life as a Coloured. He wanted to get a new identity document: one without the 'W' before and after his name and number, which indicated that he had been accepted as a member of the 'white population-group' (as it was officially referred to). He was determined to see to the matter immediately.

The word 'marriage' was uttered by neither of them. Both felt embarrassed about it.

The following day he went to the Population Registration Office and handed over his identity document. He wanted to be registered as a Coloured, he said. In order to achieve this end he had to make a formal declaration, as stipulated under the Population Registration Act. The declaration was drafted in the usual terms: Demitrios Tsafendas regarded himself as a Coloured, lived in a Coloured residential area, had the intention of entering into marriage with a woman of mixed racial origins.

The bureaucratic mills were to grind slowly over this request. At that time applications were flooding in from Coloureds who wanted to be classified as whites. Applications to change status in the other direction were rare indeed. Demitrios was one of the exceedingly small number of people who were volunteering to disadvantage themselves by crossing in this particular direction the mad, artificially imposed boundaries between races.

For six weeks he remained with the Daniels family. During that time he heard nothing from the Population Registration Office. He wondered why his reclassification was taking so long. In the meantime he had managed to get a job as a fitter in a local power station. Perhaps, Mr Daniels then suggested, he might make a contribution to the costs of the household, as their means were so limited. Demitrios now began to complain of stomach pains. At mealtimes, grimacing, he would withdraw from the table and head for his room.

Still nothing had been said about the putative marriage. At forty-seven he was quite old for Helen; she was twelve years younger. In the end, relieved that he kept silent on the subject, she decided to let the prospect of marriage between them quietly evaporate. He was a charming man, she thought, and she enjoyed listening to his opinions on various subjects, but his manners increasingly struck her as odd. At nights he would go into the kitchen and hunt around for something to eat. She had once found him on his bed with his shoes on.

'He was just lying there with his feet on the bedspread,' Helen complained. It was a fluffy, rose-coloured bedspread made of combed cotton.

During September and October of that year Demitrios went regularly to meetings of The Christian Church. These meetings took place in various houses all over the Cape Peninsula. In the whole western Cape there were about eight hundred people in the group. Their 'church' did not have a building of its own, gave out no reading matter and did not hold collections during its services. The Gospel was presented in an informal, friendly manner; the transforming power of Christ's presence was proclaimed; tea or a light supper was shared after the service. The community abided strictly by the law. In the words of one its leaders: 'Our faith caters for European and non-European races. We are not multi-racial, but we do gather with Coloured members of The Christian Church during our annual conferences. We, however, obey the apartheid laws. By this I mean that the members of different races eat and sleep separately.'

It made no difference to Demitrios whether the services he attended took place in Coloured areas or in the better-off neighbourhoods of the whites. He went back and forth between them as the spirit took him. His white fellow believers formed the impression that he came to the services for the food, chiefly. He appeared devout, but was ignorant of the texts. He sat with his hands on his knees. Sometimes his legs could be seen trembling. And he called for the discussion of strange questions. How, for instance, could

Jesus have been active in heaven before appearing in Mary's womb? He sang hymns with the enthusiasm of a child; this went down better among the Coloureds than among the whites.

One day, after a Bible reading, he was taken aside by James Johnson, a white elder of the community. This was the second time that the man had questioned him. What exactly was the colour of his skin, Johnson wanted to know. As determined from the official point of view, of course. Was he a Greek or a 'non-white'? Demitrios began to explain his circumstances. Johnson interrupted him. As long as his racial classification was officially white ('European') – surely this must be clear to him? – he should no longer go to prayer meetings in the houses of Coloureds. Nothing but trouble would come of it.

Towards the beginning of summer Demitrios left Bellville South. He wandered from one hired room to another in the city centre, and finally found himself in the southern suburbs, in Lansdowne, where a family by the name of O'Ryan offered him shelter. Patrick O'Ryan, whom he had met at one of the meetings of The Christian Church, was a teacher at the Bishop Lavis High School. He took pity on this homeless Greek. He shared with him not only his bread and his belief, but also a mixed background. It was apparent to him that Demitrios had only a limited understanding of the Bible, but for the rest he found him easy to get on with.

Demitrios remained unemployed for several weeks. He applied for a job as a concierge at the French embassy, in vain; and for a clerkship at the Groote Schuur Hospital, with the same result. Soon after the New Year he tried for a job as a conductor in the City tramways, but had no success there either – he was too plump to run all day up and down the narrow stairs of a double-decker. Then he applied to the Marine Diamond Corporation, a company with its headquarters at the harbour. On 13 January 1966 he successfully underwent a medical examination; two weeks later he was at work.

The company dredged for diamonds on the Atlantic coast. He sailed on a supply ship for a site six hundred miles north of Table Bay, at the mouth of the Orange River. He and the other workmen on board spent a night getting there; then they were transferred to a dinghy with an outboard motor. A strong southeaster was blowing. With difficulty the dinghy reached the giant pontoon on which the dredging machine was mounted. While the others were still vomiting over the railings, or were taking to their bunks below, Demitrios, exhausted though he was, went to the bathroom and made his early morning toilet.

The foreman at once decided that this man 'knew the sea'. The crew took it in turn to work in shifts of twelve hours apiece, for twenty days at a time; then they were sent away for ten days' leave in Cape Town. At first he fitted in well. Though lazy, he was seldom sick; he ate like an ox and generally slept about three hours less when off shift than the rest of the men. Together with John Hulse, a student earning money during his vacation, and an older American crewman, he maintained the pumps which sucked up the mud from the sea bottom and passed it into giant bins.

Demitrios talked non-stop while on the job; it was as if being back on the ocean, even in these circumstances, had loosened his tongue. In no time at all everyone knew all about his *Wanderjahre* and his contempt for the South African regime. He was proud of having spent time living among Malays and Coloureds. You could get on with such people, he announced; at least they had some sense. The Nationalist Party was crap; nor was it going to last long. As for the Immorality Act – which forbade love between the races – it was the Act itself that was immoral, not what it tried to prevent.

The head of security on board – a certain Keith Martincich – warned Demitrios to put more distance between himself and the black riggers and unskilled workers on board the dredger; also to keep away from the filters through which the mud was sieved. Quite apart from mud and diamonds, the pumps sucked up quantities of red lobsters. Demitrios, the seafood lover, could not keep away from such a bonanza. At free moments during the night shift he would fish about in the bins, and then, in the mornings, bring his harvest into the kitchen.

Martincich was a slightly built man of twenty-three. He decided to watch this odd fellow, and crept after him whenever he took himself to some deserted corner of the deck. To his surprise he heard the man, at these times, talking loudly to himself. It was a long monologue – or was it a dialogue? Demitrios spoke of himself as a man who had dived into the sea to rescue drowning men. He acted out the story of the Cape hero, Wolraad Woltemade, who rode on horseback to bring shipwrecked sailors ashore.

In his mind he was listening attentively once again to the English mistress at his school in Middelburg. Lost in these reveries, he clapped his hands and cried out loudly. Then he would fall silent and stare at the strip of land visible in the distance. He felt an inexplicable sadness. He longed for Mozambique, for Cora in her house of many rooms. And still further back too, for

Alexandria and his grandmother Katerina, who had always treated him so kindly. The sun went down. The mud from the broad mouth of the Orange River streamed out to sea, turning the sea-water blood-brown.

Two months later Demitrios appeared in the office of Gillian Liebermann, head of personnel for the Marine Diamond Corporation. The noise and vibration on board the great dredger had damaged his hearing, he told her. His nose was troubling him too; this was an after-effect of having had it broken six years before, in a fight in a Jerusalem slum. In Liebermann's opinion his clothing and physical appearance were not those of the average employee of the Marine Diamond Corporation. His hat and his European-style suit helped to make him something of an exception, an oddity. He struck her as a unique and imaginative person. She questioned him, listened to his stories, and found herself drawn into a prolonged conversation with him. The upshot of their meeting was an appointment with the firm's medical officer.

At the beginning of April he took two weeks' leave and was admitted into the Groote Schuur Hospital. Dr Leon Goldmann, an ear, nose and throat specialist, operated on his left nostril. Three days later he was discharged. A social worker took him from the hospital to a boarding house run by an ex-nurse in the suburb of Observatory.

Demitrios shared his room with an Afrikaans-speaking bus-driver and a German back-packer. When, at the end of one of the meals they took together, he politely thanked the black serving-maid who had served at their table, he saw the Afrikaner scowl. This led to a heated argument between them about Verwoerd, the blacks and the Bantustans supposedly being developed for them. The tension between Demitrios and his room-mate deepened over the next few days. Demitrios refused to put out his bedside lamp at night; he insisted on reading into the small hours. He slept with his money and papers hidden under his pillow. On the last day of May he told the owner of the boarding house, to her face, that the Afrikaners were a backward people. She responded by telling him to go and look for lodgings elsewhere.

He must have felt particularly hopeless during the winter of 1966. Again he went from rented room to room, in that flat stretch of the city which lies just below Devil's Peak. He applied for one menial job after another, never with any success. Now and then he went back to the Population Registration Office, to record his changes of address, so that he could be informed if his application to change his racial status had been granted. The papers, he was told, had been sent to the Ministry of the Interior in Pretoria, where they were being carefully studied. Continuous headaches and dizziness led him to seek help from a neurologist, but nothing emerged from the examination he went through. He was told that he was suffering from a form of migraine, and that he was over-weight: nothing else. The doctor sent him away with some codeine tablets and a pamphlet on slimming. Because of his gross appetite and table manners he had become notorious in the rundown cafe where he usually took his lunch, on the edge of District Six. The people working there had given him a nickname: 'The Pig'.

During one of his many visits to the labour bureau he fell into conversation with a retired railwayman. The railwayman told him that casual jobs could often be found in the Senate and House of

Assembly. As the government migrated seasonally between Cape Town and Pretoria – spending the summer on the coast and the winter on the highveld – the officials who ran the day-to-day business of parliament were always looking for temporary messengers and suchlike. The pay was poor. Such jobs should have been filled by Coloureds, really, but the dignity of parliament demanded otherwise. A temporary position there would be better than nothing, anyhow.

On Monday 18 July Demitrios appeared for a short interview in the parliament buildings. He had cut his hair for the occasion and shaved himself with especial care. He wore a grey suit. He was received in an impressive, wood-panelled office by the Chief Messenger, Mr Burger, who was accompanied by two Senior Messengers, Schuin and Wiehahn.

First of all, they told him, he must not expect to get a permanent appointment. This was for reasons he already knew. The work itself was not onerous: for the most part it consisted of sorting post and delivering messages, documents and newspapers. If he were to be appointed, he would have to be obedient to his superiors. At the end of the Cape session, in three months' time, he would be discharged. Schuin lit a cigarette. Wiehahn stirred his coffee. Burger asked him if he understood the position.

Demitrios answered that he did indeed. A number of formal questions were then rapidly put to him. Was he a South African? Could he prove that he was classified as a white? What grade had he reached at school? Who were his previous employers? When had he been discharged from their employ?

The officials examined the certificate of attendance he had

received from the Middelburg School, as well as the registration card issued by the labour bureau, on which his identity-card number (with its 'W' for white) also appeared. They listened to his account of the time he had spent working for the Marine Diamond Corporation, and did not question the reason he gave for resigning from it. ('On account of age.') Demitrios added that he had also worked at one time as a court translator in Natal.

'Did you really translate from Greek and Portuguese in front of a magistrate?' Wiehahn asked, after he had listed his languages for them. Burger, who had been watching him closely, said in Afrikaans to the other two, 'I don't think we can use someone like this as a messenger.'

Demitrios turned towards him. 'I understand what you're saying, sir. But I'm hungry. I'm desperate. I need the job.'

'You should be looking for something better,' the Chief Messenger told him. 'We have trouble with people like you.'

Burger had a poor opinion of most of those who came to his door in search of a job. A spineless lot they were. Unemployed youngsters, sacked railwaymen, marginal types. The law compelled him to appoint to these positions whites only. But what kind of whites would choose such a 'career'? Rubbish, the sweepings of the slums. Or else older and better-educated men who would take off at the first opportunity. As far as he was concerned it was the latter category to which Tsafendas belonged.

'Yes, we do have trouble with people like you,' Schuin joined in. 'You're here for a day or two and then you're gone.'

Demitrios promised that he would stay for the full three-month period.

Schuin and Wiehahn nodded politely in the direction of the

door. Tsafendas took the hint. Other applicants were waiting in the anteroom. He would be informed by post whether he had got the job or not.

Just three days later the Greek oil-tanker, *Eleni*, en route to the Persian Gulf, lost a section of its rudder. It wallowed helplessly in the Atlantic Ocean, to the south-east of the Cape of Good Hope, until a Portuguese trawler responded to Captain Michaelis Fountatos's call for help. The *Eleni* was towed into Table Bay and moored at the Duncan Dock on Sunday evening, 24 July.

Demitrios always followed carefully the column in the newspaper devoted to the comings and goings of shipping in and out of the port. On Monday evening he went on board the *Eleni*. He spent a couple of hours with the ship's cook and others, introducing himself to them as a fellow seaman. Later that evening they offered him a place at their mess-table.

The entire crew of the *Eleni* was Greek. The boat would have to spend weeks in dry dock, while its rudder was being repaired. Any diversion was welcome. Demitrios told his new-found friends about the shows in town. If they wanted to buy clothes or anything else he knew where to take them.

Thereafter he appeared on the *Eleni* for lunch every day. After all, he was a Greek among fellow Greeks once again. He accompanied members of the crew when they went ashore and introduced them to Mike Augustides, of Mike's Outfitters, who was eager to do business with them. He also took them to a bar in Woodstock, where the booze was cheap, and then to the little lanes in District Six and Walmer, where the whores plied their trade. A number of the men had visited the Cape previously, and had fond memories of the high quality of its *dagga* and the good looks of its Coloured women. But Mimis warned them to be careful. Some of the police might wink an eye at what went on, but in general magistrates dealt harshly with people brought up before them. For a white man to have sex with a Coloured woman could lead to a month or more in jail. His friends shrugged their shoulders at this. What was forbidden by day was hidden at night. Besides, one of them said, everybody knew that this Verwoerd was himself married to a Coloured woman. She had 'passed', or her mother had 'passed'. So now she was white.

The watchman on the *Eleni* was an Afrikaner by the name of Stollenkamp. He was on the *qui vive* even during the small hours of the night, when the seamen would try to smuggle their women up the gangway. 'No Coloureds on board,' he insisted fiercely.

On 1 August Demitrios took up his duties as a parliamentary messenger. Schuin and Wiehahn gave him his instructions. He was attached to the press and information division of the House. A blue uniform was issued to him, along with a set of khaki-coloured overalls and a locker in which to keep his belongings. Most of his time was passed in a basement lobby. It was there that the messengers waited. They were summoned to different rooms in the buildings by lights going on in a panel fixed to the wall. He had to take tea or coffee to members of parliament and visiting journalists and to carry bundles of papers from one place or person to another.

Thus, to his own bewilderment, Demitrios Tsafendas found himself, day after day, close to some of the most powerful people in the country: ministers, parliamentary representatives from near and far, the bigwigs of the governing Nationalist Party and the opposition. In the poorer quarters of the city anyone who was acquainted with him knew how much he detested Verwoerd and his Nationalists. Yet, through some freakish mischance, here he was, at the very centre of the country's political life. Among them. Surrounded by them. Yet as if invisible to them.

The irony of his holding a position just there, at that place and at that particular moment, was even greater than he could have known. His request to be re-registered under the Population Registration Act as a Coloured – a request he had initiated exactly eleven months previously – had been passed from office to office in the Ministry of the Interior in Pretoria until, some time in July 1966, it had been discovered that the name of the applicant actually appeared on the blacklist of those forbidden to enter South Africa. On 8 August the Secretary of the Interior submitted to his Minister a deportation order against Demitrios. The order was signed by the Minister the next day and despatched to Cape Town. On Friday 2 September, a low-ranking official in Cape Town finally got round to typing a letter informing Tsafendas that he was to be deported. The letter remained in the official's out-tray until the day of the murder.

Who can tell when Demitrios decided that he would one day have to carry out an action which would heal, or make whole, his past? Was it in Durban? Or when that Catholic priest in Mandini had accosted him?

He was sick with shame and nostalgia. Nostalgia for he knew not what. Between the women of his mind and the women he met there was a gulf that nothing could bridge. He had worn out the soles of his shoes on the streets of Cape Town, looking for companionship; but no sooner did he find anyone to talk to than another face, a face from the past, would come between himself and his interlocutor. Everything he remembered melted into everything else. It was as if someone else was walking alongside him, but always just out of step with him. Sometimes he seemed to be ahead of his companion, sometimes behind. Even the thoughts he had, his own thoughts, actually seemed to well up inside this other person. Always he felt himself to be on a journey from one place to another, or from one place which strangely substituted itself for another. Now his imaginings ran together, unstoppably, violently, indiscriminately, filling him with shame; now they put before him, with a shameless reality far stronger than anything before his eyes, precise, changeless moments from his past.

During the weekends of August he could no longer bear to go out of his room. The WC was at the end of a corridor, but it was impossible for him to negotiate even that distance. When he was sure his landlady was not around he peed into cola bottles and threw them out of the window, into the garden. He ate Cadbury's chocolate bars incessantly, one after the other, a whole bar at a time. His room was littered with their silver wrappings.

When he finally understood what he was going to do, what he had to do, when the deed he was going to commit finally made itself known to him, he felt a kind of relief. It was as if all the turmoil in his mind was suddenly stilled. In its place there came an emptiness. It was impossible for him to know whether it was agreeable or not.

What could be easier, now that he had a job in parliament? Everything was at hand. He had long believed that a firearm was the most efficient weapon a man could use to kill another. A revolver or pistol had the great advantage of striking from a distance, and of therefore allowing the assailant to escape. Previously he had had no idea what 'escape' might mean, but now that the *Eleni* lay in harbour the answer seemed clear to him. Once you were inside the parliament buildings, he knew, security was very lax. He would come on the man in one of the corridors, shoot him down, escape in the confusion that would be bound to follow, and run like hell towards the docks.

But time was getting short: it was now or never. The *Eleni* was due to sail within a few days. He had become very thick with some members of the crew. They often complained to him about the stupidity of South African laws. He allowed himself to drop some vague hints of what he had in mind and they encouraged him to go ahead; or so it seemed to him. He even gave himself a definite date on which he would carry out his plan: 2 September. Manolis, the tall bosun on the *Eleni*, had told him that he had a Beretta which he would part with for eighty dollars.

On 1 September Demitrios went to the Adderley Street branch of Barclays Bank. He produced his passport and bought as many American dollars as he needed. Then he took a taxi to the docks. He greeted the man on day watch and went below. But now that Manolis realised Demitrios was in earnest, he suddenly got cold feet. The two men began to shout at one another. Manolis took him into the kitchen, knowing that the cook's assistant, a seventeen-year-old called Nikolas Mavronas, had a small pistol he had been wanting to dispose of. He brought it out for them to look at: a black weapon with a white butt and the inscription on it: Brevettata .22 MADE IN ITALY. Mavronas did not have any ammunition for it. Mimis finally counted out thirty dollars and left the boat with the gun in his pocket.

Manolis saw him off the side and told the watchman not to let him on board again; the man was crazy. The watchman did not take this instruction seriously. The fat fellow had been coming and going all month long, without doing any harm, and was obviously on good terms with some of the men on board.

That evening, in his room in Aldor Apartments, Rondebosch, Mimis discovered that the gun was little more than a toy. It was a small-calibre gas-pistol; barely a firearm at all. He swallowed his anger as best he could. He consulted his Bible but got no guidance from it.

The following day he carried out in a distracted fashion the jobs he was given to do. Sent into town to despatch a message for one of the parliamentary correspondents, he came back with the wrong change. That evening the press corps gave its annual party for members of both the Senate and the House of Assembly. Demitrios was asked to help out as a waiter. One of the guests at the party was John Hulse, a member of the Students Representative Council at Cape Town University, who was a friend of an opposition M.P. He recognised Demitrios and greeted him warmly. They'd worked together on that dredger: didn't he remember? Demitrios gave him an evasive answer.

On Saturday 3 September he went on board the *Eleni* for the last time. He wanted to get back his thirty dollars. Either that or another gun. Or even a proper knife. Manolis and the cook's assistant told him that they'd spent the money and it was too late now to ask for it back.

'Piss off,' the bosun said. 'What do you think we are, a couple of cowboys?'

Nevertheless Demitrios ate in the galley with them and some others. At three o'clock he went on to the bridge, where Michaelis Fountatos was preparing for the boat's departure. He complained to the captain that he'd been swindled; but the captain simply hustled him off the bridge. He should settle his own accounts with the men below.

At six o'clock that evening the ropes that moored the *Eleni* to the quay were cast off.

*

At a quarter to seven on the morning of Tuesday 6 September – it was a clear spring day – Demitrios took up his position in the lobby of the House of Assembly. He was expected on duty only an hour later, and he occupied himself with the morning newspapers. During the weekend Verwoerd had had a meeting with Chief Leaboa Jonathan, the leader of Basutoland, a former British Protectorate. Today, at two, the Prime Minister was expected to report on this meeting, and to make an important statement on the future of the Bantustans. Parliament would be full, Mimis knew. Almost all the members would want to be present, not to speak of members of the public seeking admission to the gallery.

But there was no way back for him.

He left for the city centre before nine. In one shop, William Rawbone's, he bought a dagger. Five minutes later, in City Guns,

Hout Street, he bought another, larger knife. The owner of City Guns took him to be a fisherman or a sailor and asked no questions of him. He wandered over to Greenmarket Square and fifteen minutes later returned to his post in the messengers' waiting-room. No one had noticed his absence. By the time he resumed his usual place, he had deposited the knives in his locker. He had tied their scabbards to a belt which he concealed under his blue uniform jacket. Then he served tea to the reporters, in their room on the first floor.

By two o'clock, just before the bell rang for the sitting to begin, the crowd that had gathered under the portico of the building was even bigger than he had expected it to be. Some four hundred people were heading for the House of Assembly, among them the final-year students of the Afrikaans-medium school, Du Preez Hoërskool, in the city's northern suburbs. Mimis went downstairs to pick up his knives and secrete them under his jacket.

At ten past two Verwoerd made his appearance. He was accompanied by his personal bodyguard, Lieutenant Colonel Buytendag, and his private secretary. Demitrios stood among the crowd in the entrance, fumbling with his jacket as Verwoerd passed by. He followed the crowd into the House of Assembly. Buytendag turned and went up into the gallery. In a moment the Prime Minister would take his seat on the benches.

Demitrios approached him. He had finally managed to free one of his knives from its scabbard. He leaned forward. People assumed that he had a message to give to Verwoerd. Then he struck. His entire weight went into the blow. The blade disappeared in Verwoerd's chest; it had been buried right up to the hilt. The premier's upper body rose; it was a reflex response merely, not a defensive movement. Demitrios remained motionless for a moment, leaning over. He pulled the knife out. It could now be seen by the people around him. He stabbed the man in front of him yet again, three more times, before he was overpowered by the bystanders.

Everyone was screaming. A group of men had thrown the murderer on the floor. He was dragged over the benches, struck, stamped on, kicked.

Dr Matthys Venter, a dominee of the Dutch Reformed Church and the M.P. for Kimberley District, was holding Demitrios's right arm. The knife was still clenched in his fist. With something more than a clergyman's strength, Venter managed to force his fingers open and took the weapon from him. While others struggled to hold the assassin, he carefully laid the knife on the Speaker's table. P.W. Botha, already a cabinet minister and later to become State President, rushed over to Helen Suzman, the solitary representative in parliament of the Progressive Party. His eyes bulging, his arms flailing, he thrust his fat forefinger in her face. 'It's you who did this!' he shouted. 'It's you liberals! Now we'll get you! We'll get the lot of you!'

Verwoerd's lifeless body was removed to the Groote Schuur Hospital. An autopsy would have to be held in order formally to establish the cause of death. To all intents and purposes the Prime Minister had died at the moment of attack. He had stab wounds in his right shoulder, his right upper arm and between the ribs; one of the thrusts had pierced his lung to a depth of thirteen centimetres and entered the right chamber of his heart.

Tsafendas was taken in a police van directly to the police station in Caledon Square, around the corner from the parliament buildings.

At a quarter to three, and at the request of the police, he was examined by the District Surgeon, Dr R. Kossew. Demitrios had sustained bruised ribs and a cut along his eyebrow and the bridge of his nose. His shirt was covered with blood. Looking at him more closely, the doctor realised that his nose was broken; also that he had seen this man before. Two months previously he had come to see him in connection with an application for a war pension. He had then thought him to be in a manifestly unstable state. Indeed, though he was not a psychiatrist, Kossew had jotted down the word 'schizophrenic' in his notes.

Eventually Demitrios followed the Prime Minister's corpse to Groote Schuur. The wound on his brow was stitched up and his nose was put in plaster. He was also given an anti-tetanus injection.

Four hours after the attack he was taken into the office of Dr Sakinofsky, the hospital's head of psychiatry.

There were just three people in the room, Dr Sakinofsky, his assistant, and Demitrios. Sakinofsky asked him to lie down and to try to relax.

Could he remember what had happened? Was it true that he had killed the Prime Minister?

Demitrios looked at him with an air of surprise. 'I don't remember what happened afterwards; but yes, I did stab him right through.'

'What made you do a thing like that?'

'I didn't agree with the policy . . .'

Demitrios sat up. He put his face in his hands and burst into tears. He cried for some time. A flood of words, of broken sentences, followed. The doctor could make sense of few of them.

'Why are you crying?' he asked at one point.

'I don't know.'

'Aren't you pleased with what you've done?'

'Yes. I'm glad to speak to you . . . someone better class. I'm always among the poorer class of people.'

Sakinofsky asked him about his background. He listened attentively to the story Demitrios began to tell him.

'Why have you never married?'

Demitrios looked embarrassed; he even blushed. 'I was working in a defence plant in Johannesburg when the war broke out. Then I joined an Allied convoy. I was very weak. I broke down after three months at sea. I didn't know then that I was troubled in my nerves . . . I see things, because of high blood pressure, coils and springs in front of my eyes. I hear no voices.'

'Does God speak to you sometimes?'

Demitrios shook his head.

'Not personally. Only when I am in bed, fast asleep. Then I feel something that passes me by.'

'Are your thoughts normal?'

'They are too rapid. In Portugal they brainwashed me and put alternating current in my head. Since then I have lost my faculties.'

'Who are you against now?'

'I'm against Verwoerd. He's a foreigner . . . He is a Nationalist and he hasn't got the people behind him. I see no progress for the African people. There *is* something spiritual in me . . . I thought this thing had gone too far, they have made an ideology of it. The sexual part of it too – the Immorality Act, telling you who you can't marry . . . The only girl who wanted to marry me did not have the right identity card. I could not keep changing my identity card.'

Then, after a short pause, 'What do they actually say over the radio about the Prime Minister?'

'That he was stabbed to death in parliament.'

'I remember stabbing him.'

Sakinofsky noted that Demitrios answered his questions spontaneously. He seemed to look at what had happened from a distance; as if astonished that he had done something that had created such an uproar.

'What did you feel when you committed the murder?'

'Nothing. I just went blank.'

7   KRUGERSDORP: THIRTY YEARS LATER

THE EUPHORIA PRODUCED by South Africa's first truly national election in 1994 – an election in which all races took part on equal terms – did not last long. Yes, a degree of human dignity had at last been restored to the country's blacks. But it soon began to dawn on them that their poverty was not going to be done away with, nor were the glaring disparities between the level of housing and health care available to them and those enjoyed by most whites. As for the Coloureds, they feared that a black African government might treat them with as much contempt as had their white masters of yesteryear. Among the whites a reluctant optimism and a feeling of collective guilt gave way to amnesia, indifference, defeatism. The hope that violence would cease – now that the politics of the country were so changed – was soon belied. In the countryside, larger numbers of Afrikaner farmers were being murdered than ever before; in the cities, where random killings went on unabated, it was as if 'the struggle' had never ended. Indeed, so far from being over, it seemed that the revolution which had been feared or dreamed of for so long was only now beginning.

Thirty years after the murder of Verwoerd I found myself in Krugersdorp, a gold-mining town about fifty kilometres west of Johannesburg. Walking down the main street, I thought to myself: well, it had to happen. The harvest of the last many years had been gathered. The self-confidence of the whites had simply broken; in public at least. Or so it appeared. They looked shabbier than before, the blacks smarter. Perhaps this impression sprang from the dress and carriage of each group, as it went about its business. The whites I saw in Krugersdorp, barely an hour's drive from Johannesburg, wore hideously ugly shorts, acrylic shirts, baseball caps with dirty peaks. Some of them even went barefoot. They slouched along, without style, without self-regard. Did they imagine that this lack of decorum signified some kind of 'sportiness'? Or was this what 'going native' entailed? Or did it spring simply from a degree of poverty new to them? Yet the blacks around them, who were poorer still, did not create the same impression. They tried to dress up, not down as the whites did. For the blacks there appeared to be something festive about going to the city centre – hence their lacquered shoes, Victorian hats, party dresses, striped trousers and suits, bright umbrellas. The last of these items gave warning of the thunderstorm that would break out later in the day; such storms came regularly in the summer afternoons, here in Gauteng (formerly known as the Transvaal).

As if from long ago, from the old, old days, 'poor whites' had reappeared. They looked exactly like those I could remember only too well from the districts next to the suburban railway lines of my youth. In Krugersdorp they lived in an industrial area to the west of the town; their dilapidated rows of little houses ran alongside a polluted tributary of the Magalies River. The whole area stank of chemicals. All Afrikaans-speaking, all unemployed, all dependent on welfare handouts, they were rich only in the numbers of their children. But for how long, in the new South Africa, could they be sure of receiving regularly their benefit payments? They were precisely the people whom apartheid had privileged; now they glanced around shiftily – lost, not knowing what to look for next, or where to look for it. They had been abandoned, here in Africa.

The old magistrates' court had been turned into a modest museum. Laid out as if in a series of shop windows were a variety of predictable items: geological specimens, mining gear, souvenirs of the Anglo-Boer War. (In the year 1900 about a thousand Boer women and children had died near the town, in one of the concentration camps set up by the British.) At the back, on a window sill, stood four bronze heads which made a deeper impression on me than all the other objects on display: the dust-covered heads of successive leaders of the Nationalist Party. There they were, Prime Ministers all, in their day: Hannes Strydom, Hendrik Verwoerd, B.J. Vorster, P.W. Botha.

Thirty years had passed since the second of these had been assassinated. What remained of that event now? After almost three decades of imprisonment in Pretoria, Tsafendas had been removed to a psychiatric hospital some ten kilometres distant from the little museum where I stood gazing at the portrait, cast in bronze, of his victim. Would it be possible to visit him? My fax to the Sterkfontein Hospital had been addressed to – ah! the irony of the conjunction! – to a Dr Botha, the director, and to a Dr Vorster, the chief physician. Now I had to wait for a few days: *killing time* in Krugersdorp.

Saturday afternoon. Inside the hotel bar. Four fans turning above the pool table. The Rolling Stones emanating from the sound system. The room dark; the conversations loud.

A young woman turns and shouts at me, 'I want to go barefoot, but just look at this filthy floor!' She has her arm around the shoulder of a man whose blue jeans hang below his belly. Below the cleft of his bottom too.

She says: 'I was seventeen when I had my first baby. It died. Then came this Boer, I went with this Boer. I was eighteen and I had his baby, the fucking arsehole, and at twenty still another one. If he gives me another baby I'm going to sell it for fucking *money*.'

The girl behind the counter undoes the buttons of her blouse, to loud applause. She laughs at us, delighted with her success. The man with the exposed bum heads towards the WC. The young mother turns to me again.

'Ach, pardon me,' she says. 'I just can't find a man worth loving. All they know is to stick it in and pump, stick it in and pump.'

Stick it in and pump? From the window of my room on the second floor of the hotel I could see the line of hills behind which, I knew, the Sterkfontein Hospital lay. I felt that down in the Cape I would have known better how large or small was my chance of succeeding in my mission. In the Transvaal everything was different, on a bigger scale, less accessible. It was almost like being in another country, one that had little or nothing in common with what I had left behind. For Transvaalers, of course, things were exactly the other way around. Table Mountain looked unreal to them, the blue of the Cape skies was like a curse.

Now that my obsession with Tsafendas was coming to its denouement, I could no longer remember where it had begun. A long time ago I had already decided that actually I had little to ask of the aged Demitrios. Nevertheless I felt a shrinking from the prospect of seeing him, a fear of doing so, as if I was about to step into icy water. Seventy-eight years old, for many years maltreated and tormented in Pretoria Central Gaol – the warders, I knew, used to spit in his food and piss in his coffee – what he deserved now, what I could perhaps offer him, was a little friendship of the Greek kind: they called it *paréa*. A handshake, a walk in the garden of the institution, a few calming words, nothing more.

Early on Monday morning I picked up the phone and called the hospital. After speaking to a few intermediaries I was put through to Dr Vorster. Yes, she had received my fax. Her voice was neutral, distant. I told her, in Afrikaans, that I had been informed by the Ministry of Justice that permission from the medical authorities was necessary before a visit to Tsafendas could be made. Was that correct? Dr Vorster coolly switched over to English. Yes, the decision was in the hands of the hospital and in principle there was no objection. But they could not agree to my coming to see him now.

Then, with an unmistakeable firmness of tone: 'He is physically in no state to receive visitors.'

Dr Vorster proved to be as good as her word. No objection was made to my application to see the patient when I tried again eighteen months later. Demitrios's health had improved. I travelled from Amsterdam with a fax in my pocket: 'Visit to Mr Tsafendas approved. Please contact Matron Geyer to confirm date and time.' An hour after the arrival of my plane in Johannesburg, I was back in my room in that Krugersdorp hotel. I phoned the hospital immediately, only to learn that Matron Geyer had already gone home for the day. So I left a message to say that I would call her again the following day.

That night I stayed in my room and watched television. Thirty-eight years earlier, to the day, a famous uprising against apartheid – the fiercest and most widespread the country had yet seen – had begun in the township of Sharpeville. In the course of a single morning sixty-seven blacks had been shot dead in that small town. Now the event was memorialised under the title of Human Rights Day. President Mandela appeared on the screen, along with Vice-President Mbeki, attending a commemorative ceremony held somewhere upcountry. The Afrikaans poet Breyten Breytenbach, who had himself undergone imprisonment and exile for what he had written and done as an opponent of the apartheid regime, succeeded the politicians on the screen. Human rights, he said, included language rights, which meant that Afrikaners were entitled still to express themselves in Afrikaans. Then it was the turn of Matthews Phosa, the eccentric premier of the province of Mpumulanga (formerly the Eastern Transvaal). He

expressed outrage at the fact that the head of state, President
Mandela, had been subpoenaed to give evidence in a court case
involving the management committee of the South African
Rugby Union. Trivial, stupid intrigues of that sort must be halted,
Phosa insisted.

They all seemed alike to me. Mbeki, Breytenbach, Phosa, the
President – they had all been exiles in their time. At least they
could all be thought of as such, provided that Mandela's years of
imprisonment on Robben Island were regarded as a form of ban-
ishment. They had all been scarred by long, enforced absences
from the country, which had been followed by a sudden return to
it: to a place which in the intervening years had itself undergone
far-reaching processes of transformation, even of dissolution. And
there was something else they had in common: for all the differences between them, they all spoke in a manner which seemed to
me recognisably South African. Recognisably patriarchal too. Their
words were delivered with a biblical weight which people elsewhere could no longer readily adopt. Only Mbeki spoke with
some hesitation, allowing long, haphazard pauses to interrupt his
delivery.

At the end of the transmission there was a news flash from
Cape Town. It was a report of a fight between two Cape Coloured
street-gangs on the Waterfront, in Cape Town. One of the gangs
was a vigilante outfit which called itself PAGAD (People Against
Gangsterism and Drugs); the name of the other was not given.
Two people had been killed; their bodies were shown, swathed in
blood-drenched sheets. Rain could be seen in the background; visible too was the silhouette of Devil's Peak, washed by the
downpour. Beloved Devil's Peak.

What was it that a friend had told me, when I had last been there, as we drove through the rain towards the university?

'You know the difference between a neurotic and a psychotic? Henkie-man, a neurotic builds castles in the air. A psychotic lives in them.'

8   A WORLD OF GLASS

THE NEXT MORNING the sky was like an immense, gleaming, oppressive dome stuck over the town. The weather forecast gave warning of a temperature of 36°C later in the day; there would be no breeze to mitigate it. Nevertheless, as I headed northwards in the taxi that was taking me in the direction of the hills and the hospital beyond them, the stillness of the atmosphere became less stifling. The heat began to feel weightless somehow. The glow in the air thinned towards the horizon, as if you were looking into a dusty crystal.

The institution was a closed one. Fiercely so. A fence of a special, South African-style barbed wire, adorned with lancet-sharp blades, ran all around it. Then came a second fence, also several metres high. Between the two fences more barbed wire had been spread out horizontally, to fill in the space. Uniformed guards at the gate inspected us morosely and checked the vehicle. I had to enter my name into a register, and to give my contact and the purpose of my visit. On the other side of the double fence many brick bungalows were randomly scattered among trees, each at a distance from the others. The roadway curved between them. People wandered over the slopes in escorted groups. White-uniformed nurses, scattered like scraps of paper against the green grass, kept to the shade.

Mr Tsafendas, I was told in the front office of a bare administrative building, was to be found in Ward 12B. The sister-in-charge would show me the way; she would not be long. When she came into the office Matron Geyer stretched out a friendly hand to me; for some reason her handshake made me feel a little shy. But there was no need for me to say anything to her. She led me to her car. As we walked together she told me that a dance for the patients was going to take place that evening. Ooh-la-la, when they had a party you had to go into hiding. Most of the patients were black; most of them were pleasant enough. The dances were big occasions for them; they really looked forward to each one. They turned up the sound system so loudly you felt your ears would burst, you'd do anything to get out of the room. Anyway the smoke alone would drive you out of it.

Mrs Geyer said all this cheerfully and spontaneously, with no hint of disapproval or patronage in her voice. I thought better of asking her exactly what kind of 'smoke' she had in mind.

Ward 12B was a barrack-like building, divided into a number of dim, echoing rooms. We went down a long corridor at the end of which were a vestibule and a little reception office. I was shown into the latter. It contained four chairs grouped around a low table. A recess panelled in hardwood had a framed text stuck on one wall: the words of an oath written by Florence Nightingale. 'I solemnly pledge,' I read, 'before God and in the presence of this assembly to practise my life in purity . . .' The rest was hidden behind a yucca plant in a pot. A little table in a corner near the window bore an expiring fern. The place smelled of Lysol and old meals and of something unpleasant and difficult to identify. Fortunately the door was open.

'Is it all right if we go for a walk in the garden?' I asked.

Mrs Geyer smiled. 'I'm afraid you'll find it difficult.'

Tsafendas had been seriously ill the previous year, she told me. Pretty close to the wire. His condition now . . . well, I'd see for myself soon. He had very few visitors and nobody could get through to him. His hearing was poor. Not long ago some television crew had come to see him. Was I connected with the television? Was there any information I needed?

'I just want to see him. To keep him company.'

Matron Geyer promised to bring me a cup of tea.

'He cries a lot, sometimes,' she added. 'When they show him photos he cries like anything.'

Once again I felt nervous, wound up, seized by doubt about my presence here. For this I blamed the yucca. And that smell. I was an intruder; nothing more.

When Demitrios was brought into the room a few moments later, this feeling left me as rapidly as it had come. One of the sturdy nurses pushed a table to one side, rolled a chair on little wheels towards me and then, in a loud voice, invited us both to sit down.

What a fine head of snow-white hair!

Demitrios's head was tilted to one side. He glanced at me, as if from an angle; his eye was placatory; his air perplexed. It was midday. Perhaps he had just eaten, and was ready for a nap.

I shouted at him, in English, 'Pleased to meet you.'

He was wearing a light-blue T-shirt, with L-O-N-D-O-N printed across it. He was dressed below in a pair of jogging trousers, bright green in colour, with white stripes running down the sides of the legs. His stomach showed through the gap between his shirt and trousers. His feet were thrust into narrow, ill-fitting, down-at-heel slippers.

Matron Geyer returned with a Coca-Cola; she apologised to me for not bringing the tea she had promised; there was none to be had. Demitrios followed her movements as she put the glass down on the side table. He was not allowed to have sweet drinks, she told me. He was overweight and his heart was not strong.

As soon as she left he whispered to me: 'You know what they always say. It's the environment. That's what we've discovered. The environment . . .' He made a sweeping gesture with his right arm. 'And what it makes of everyone. Anyone you like, in the whole world, the whole world . . .'

His pronunciation of English struck me as odd; I had not imagined that it would sound like this. The intonation was old-fashioned; he had an archaically *middle-class* accent that took me back to my childhood. I might almost have been listening – had I closed my eyes – to one of the adults I used to hear in those days. Or to a good-natured fatty from one of the British children's books I used to read. Or from one of the long-forgotten, pre-war weekly comics: *The Gem*, *The Magnet*, something of that sort.

But if his vocabulary had fossilised thirty years before, his sweet tooth was what it always had been.

His hand moved compulsively towards the cool drink. He leaned towards me. 'Do you mind?'

I offered him the glass. He emptied it in one long gulp. He gave a hiccup.

'By the way,' he asked, 'where do you live? Hopetown? Rustenberg?'

'Holland,' I shouted shamelessly in his ear. '*Ollandia*!'

But it didn't get through to him.

'Thank you very very much,' he replied.

Evidently Demitrios assumed that I had come to listen to him, and without further ado or encouragement he launched himself into the middle of a stream of consciousness or free association, as if sharing recollections with an old acquaintance.

'I've always done whatever I wished. The northern seas, during the war, mountains of stone and ice. It was frightful. I went past the Isle of Stromboli with a ship. The volcano, a live volcano, a brilliant sight.'

'And the Isle of Crete?' I shouted back at him.

'Ach, I was there too. It was very old, dilapidated. But I liked the technology of Turkey. Very good dentistry too. Solid gold. They make bridges that last forever.'

He was rubbing his right hand over his left arm, which rested on his upper leg. He was lame on the left side, I thought; hence a certain sluggishness, too, in the movement of his tongue.

'The speed of life in the United States of America is terrific. And the noise! Because of mass production, do you see?' he said enthusiastically. And a moment later: 'One thing we have here in Africa, we have time to think, lots of time. We realise now that the environment is stronger than anything. We've got to give Darwin the credit. Darwin's *Evolution of the Species* was an exceptional contribution.

'Look at the motor car,' he went on. 'One day they'll be driving big black cars just on sunlight. From the sun's rays they'll drive at seventy-five miles an hour.'

Demitrios laughed. Then he sighed. I remained looking at him attentively. Because of his deafness I guessed that he would draw as much from my gaze as from any words that might get through to him. I was surprised by the absence of suspicion in his manner; also that he should have plainly wanted to reward or oblige me for having come to see him. We sat closely together, myself and a man whom I had known for so long from papers only, whose appearance and manner I had drawn from the archives and filled out from my imagination. Now here he was; and here I was, next to him. I felt that the picture I had formed of him over those years had not after all been so distant from the reality I found. Or at any rate it was distant in one regard only: he was more agreeable than I had expected him to be. He could almost have been my father. The two men were of the same age: both had been born in 1918. Unwillingly I found myself comparing them. They were both oldest sons who had left home early. Both became emigrants; wanderers, in fact. Both were deeply dissatisfied with themselves, two dreamers who longed to be men of action. But thereafter the comparison went awry. It was out of the differences between them that I had constructed my image of Tsafendas.

I could put it to myself only in an understated fashion. From his earliest days Demitrios must have been far more desperate. Must have felt himself cherished incomparably less.

My thoughts had wandered away, and Demitrios knew it. He began to speak telegraphically once again, in short sentences, some of them consisting of hardly more than a single word, with a heavy emphasis on the consonants.

'We had this huge place in Lourenço Marques, this meeting place for Greeks. They came there to speak to each other in High Greek. Ah, Crete. My father was born in Crete, during the Turkish Ottoman empire. The Turks used to rule over most of the islands in those days. My father was a special drinker of Turkish coffee. He taught me how to boil it . . . He used to sing in Turkish. He smoked Greek cigarettes, Venizelos brand . . .'

Occasionally he would let his head drop tiredly, and then raise it again. He embarked on a long monologue in the course of which he spoke of such harbours as Herakleion, Chania, Piraeus, Lourenço Marques. Then, without any link between the one subject and the next, he was talking of Greek architecture. And that led him back to the Greek community in Lourenço Marques.

'I want to make a mausoleum there, with the assistance of the people who built the big buildings. They were Greeks, all of them. The Akropolis, the department store. The St George. Big. Out of nothing. The man who built the Akropolis had rickshaw boys working for him' – he laughed briefly at the memory – 'terribly slowly, brick by brick. And underneath, all shops. They made a *city* out of Lourenço Marques.

'Those Greeks were very conservative. My biological mother wanted me to go further with Greek history. She influenced me. She was a very cosmopolitan woman. She spoke French quite well. I wish I could see her now. They lived, the last time I saw them, in Proclamation Hill, Pretoria. And the City Tearoom, Quagga Road.'

He yawned. I waited. When he resumed he again confused his natural mother with Marika, his stepmother. It was plain to me that they had not merged with one another in his mind, after all these years. The distinction between them had remained clear. But he had exchanged their identities and names, one for the other. Just as I, I found myself thinking, had always believed the wound inflicted on him in Natal to have been on his left arm. But it was his right arm that carried the scar. Elsewhere his skin was fine in texture, almost hairless, surprisingly smooth for a man of eighty.

'That wound,' he said thoughtfully. 'I no longer remember exactly what happened. I was stabbed in Port Shepstone. What a job it was to sew it up! They operated to join the tendons. They wanted to give me an anaesthetic. I refused . . . I went to Stuttafords to have a cup of tea, tea with toast. I'll never forget the rickshaws in Durban. Do you still remember the rickshaws in Durban?'

Matron Geyer put her head around the corner. Was everything all right? Yes, fine. Demitrios and I sat and smiled at one another, the old man still holding forth, I responding with nods.

'We Greeks were rivals against the orientals. Very strong rivals. They brought me up very strict against the orientals, the Arabs especially . . . I was taken out of the French mission school. I was learning the black language there, Shangaan. It was a big mistake. They should have left me but they sent me to a Catholic Portuguese school. And from there they took me out again and sent me to school in Middelburg, in the Transvaal. I had difficulty because of Afrikaans in one class and English in the other. I didn't know Afrikaans. But I kept on, I persisted, I had no choice because my parents were so strict.

'I had a big tooth pulled out there by a dentist called de Villiers. That tooth made history. He couldn't yank it out. I was sitting in the hall with all the other children and they were laughing. He got angry and chased them out of the room. It was *big*, the root. All night I was losing blood on my pillow. That was in Nelson House, the school hostel. When I visited London the first thing I wanted to visit was Nelson's *Victory*. And when I went there I signed my name in the book. The guard said: "Put your address there, sign your name . . ."'

He told the story with evident satisfaction, proud that the man had asked him for his signature. If he had been somewhat subdued initially, he was now animated, alert, carried away by his own words. He spoke about his childhood days in Alexandria and the house of his grandmother Tsafandakis. He had long had in his possession a photograph of himself as a little boy, in Arab garb.

'I kept it. I put it in an envelope when I was in Pretoria Central prison. Potgieter, he destroyed it. It disappeared there. I used to keep it, but Potgieter the chief warder destroyed it, also my birth certificate. I had all that. I knew it was historic. But Potgieter was against me, he tore everything up. It would make history, but that stupid Potgieter . . .'

He trailed off, agitatedly, weeping. Over the following days he repeatedly complained about that incident.

'Potgieter was *furious* against anything that belonged to me. But his helper was very good to me. I'd like to see him. He sympathised with me and protected me whenever possible, when I was beaten on the skull. Blood used to come! He was also an Afrikaner, but different . . .

'Completely different, very good-natured,' he repeated.

A little later, clearly referring still to the prison in Pretoria, he said: 'I'd like to go back there, where I used to live in that building. It's been transformed into a holy place now. A *hóóóly* place. You must find out. You must enquire.'

Outside a light breeze had begun to blow over the lawns of Sterkfontein. I had spent hours in his presence. His recollections were fragmented in a manner that was peculiarly his own. The Greek-African story-teller.

Scrabbling through the dislocations of time, confined within the barrier of his defective hearing, he picked up tiny moments of his memories, like bits of stone, and then let them drop. The longer I listened, however, the more I began to suspect that his manner of jumping from topic to topic was also a way of testing me, perhaps to find out how much I knew of his history. Was he then merely playing games? No, not always, and not with any definite aim, but still – Demitrios gave the impression of being someone who was used to improvising with whatever he retained of his own past. As if he had often been compelled to go through it. Or as if the film of his existence consisted of hundreds of rushes that still had to be finally put together. So he was free to edit them differently, each time.

At one point he began to sing to me English songs from fifty and more years ago – *for old times' sake*, he said, the spittle flying out of the corner of his mouth as he said the phrase. By now he had become positively elated. Among the songs was 'A Bicycle Made for Two' ('Daisy, Daisy . . .'). Drawing long breaths he also burst into a hymn I remembered from my schooldays: 'Onward Christian Soldiers/Marching as to war/With the cross of Jesus/Going on before . . .'

Weeks later the smell of that visit was still with me. It was the smell of old, unwashed men. The rotten sweetness of uncared-for teeth and unwashed armpits, mixed with the odours of half-digested food rising from the bowels and through the pores of the skin. Demitrios was a neglected creature. That was the truth. Matron Geyer was not to be blamed. There was nothing that she could do about it. The hospital was hopelessly understaffed.

Just before I left he asked, 'Are you an enthusiast of flying?'

The question was wonderfully dated. It belonged, I thought, to an era of golfing caps and plus fours on English greens: it was a question that polite young men might have asked each other on first getting acquainted, in 1928 say, when you could not take for granted the prospect of travelling by air. Or, for that matter, when you did not know if your acquaintances were regular listeners to that other newfangled contraption, 'the wireless'.

As I got up to go he made me promise to return the next day.

Back in the hotel in Krugersdorp. The Afrikaner cowboys and cow-girls were still hanging around in the bar. Weak with hunger, I went into the dining-room. I was the only guest, waited on by a girl who from time to time fiddled with the hem of her mini-skirt. Music came incessantly out of the speakers on the walls, as numbingly as ever. The walls, the ceiling and the carpet in the room were green; so were the table cloths. But not any old green: this was a dark, alpine-hat green, with here and there, by way of contrast, a hint of sombre red. I was eating in a green-red womb, under the sign of romance, Transvaal-style. By which I mean the two exaggeratedly blue and violet paintings, landscapes both, hung on the walls. One showed a gilded ship daintily stranded on rocks; the other a blood-curdling sunset seen through a thorn bush, while two buck and a rhino drank at a nearby pool.

My thoughts were still in Sterkfontein. The meeting had left me feeling dizzy. I had come assuming that I would meet an extinguished human being. Someone whose illness could only have been exacerbated by three decades of imprisonment and maltreatment. A man whom witnesses had described after the attack, almost without exception, in wholly unsympathetic terms: a pig, a liar, a nutcase. And surely, after his 'release', I would find him infantile, deaf, manifestly crazy.

What I had found, instead, was a charming chatterbox. A survivor from the detritus of South African history.

Why was he still confined in the wretched institution in which I had found him? Between 1942 and 1963 alone – his period abroad – he had been arrested five times, deported five times, twice incarcerated for long periods, and eight times refused entry into South Africa. During the fifties and sixties he had regarded himself as a kind of pilgrim, that much was clear. A man with a mission, even if he could never have said exactly where his Mecca lay. Now that everything was long behind him, he remained one of the few among the huge band of exiles who had never been able to come home again, both literally and metaphorically.

Most people know how to give their past a form that seems plausible to themselves and others. We tell and re-tell a chronologically ordered story, and seldom lose the knack of giving to particular incidents within that story – the successive events of childhood, say, physical or spiritual traumas, the loss of parents or loved ones – more emphasis than others. We have put them in line, so to speak. Demitrios had never managed it. There was no such line in his consciousness. He was incapable of arranging his past, or even of separating it from the present. The connections he did make were not chronological but mythical. Almost any incident of his life could be enlarged or coloured as he wished, as if he looked at himself through some strange lens which dissociated him from the everydayness of his psyche. In a sense he had acquired the gift of a sophisticated story-teller: he looked on time as an ever changing substance, or as nothing more than a hypothesis that might be abandoned here or there, depending on its effect, or which was controlled by a higher allegorical meaning. But for Demitrios this habit must have often been a pain rather than a pleasure; a source of torment to him.

That afternoon, sitting next to an old man comprehensively saying his piece (and willingly too, as if he might never have another chance to do it), I had felt myself to be endowed with an unwonted perspicacity. No doubt his stories sounded like concoctions to those who knew little or nothing of his background. For him all he had ever been, all he could ever speak of, was secluded within a domain of glass, isolated, viewable only as if through a lens scored by sharp cracks and flaws.

In the green dining-room of that hotel in Krugersdorp I asked myself if I knew of a better way of trying to apprehend the history of his country.

'Please let's go somewhere,' he said by way of greeting the next morning. 'I don't know where I am. Everything looks so strange to me. Can I go into the sunshine? Obtain some sunshine?'

The hefty nurse I had seen yesterday walked past.

'*Haai*, Mr Tsafendas.' He hit Demitrios good-humouredly on the back, and stretched out his dark hand in an African-style greeting, taking the patient's hand by the palm and then by the thumb.

'Ah, the Strong Man,' Demitrios answered, saying the last words as if they were a name rather than a description. Then, to me: 'He's a really good chap. A very virtuous man. But Strong.'

We were sitting in the same room as before. Today Demitrios was wearing a striped polo shirt with white buttons. STERK-FONTEIN HOSPITAL 12B had been written with a felt-tip pen in crooked letters across it. He spoke more clearly than he had previously, and was more emotionally affected by what he was saying. The stories came out as if he had spent far too long in solitude. But as for the topics they touched on: they were what they had always been.

'My biological mother was a strong woman. Not very big but well proportioned – an athletic figure. Her face was full of small-pox holes. She had a sister. I love her sister. I'm in love with her. Very delicate and amusing. But she married this Greek wrestler, a champion from the United States. He was muscle-bound. They did not match. She got sick, she nearly died. She was so delicate and angelic. I loved her, till today. But this man . . . He was cheated into coming to Africa by his relations. He owned a biscuit bakery, he specialised in pastry and some kinds of sweets and chocolates. It was a mistake this aunt of mine made, marrying that wrestler.'

Then, looking around for the attendant, 'And where's the Strong Man? Where is he?'

He rubbed his trouser leg, lifting with some difficulty his paralysed left leg over his right knee.

'He's very virtuous. Healthy, too, the Strong Man. But where is he? I'm searching for my false teeth . . . Oh *ja*, they're in the washroom.'

The Strong Man returned with a plate of food: rice, spinach, beef cut into small pieces. While I held the plate for him, Demitrios fed himself with a plastic hospital spoon. He stuffed the food into his mouth but chewed each mouthful thoroughly. Eventually, working earnestly and systematically, he succeeded in emptying the plate. With the rim of his spoon he gathered the remaining grains of rice. Some of them spilled while he was eating, so I brushed them off his lap and shook them off his shirt.

After lunch his thoughts veered off on another tack. 'I wanted to have strong children. So I restrained myself from women. I kept myself chaste. No smoking, nothing. Working all the time. No whisky drinking. Milk shakes I drink, Coca-Cola and Pepsi-Cola. In Egypt we have a special drink from sugarcane, I don't remember what they call it. And pineapples. Water melon. Sweetmelon.'

He fell silent.

I wrote on the pad: WAS THERE A WOMAN IN YOUR LIFE?

He read the question slowly, as if spelling it out letter by letter.

It did not seem to dismay him. On the contrary, he set about answering it like a conscientious autobiographer, from the very beginning.

'The first woman in my life, I was young, I was under age. She was Portuguese and I used to go with her. She said to me, "What do you like? Do you want to copulate or do you want me to suck you off?" I said to her, "I want to copulate. I want to push." I was very small . . .'

He laughed, relieved and amused at the memory. 'I remember she was living in a house and next door was Gregoris. He was the Greek making ice cream, he used to sell ice cream to the city. I used to go and speak to Gregoris, then I met this woman.'

'And in Cape Town?' I asked.

'No, I did not know any woman in Cape Town. In Istanbul, yes, I had a girlfriend in Turkey. She was very intelligent. She got me the job in the college as a professor of English. She spoke to the authorities. And in Athens, one of the Greek girls in my church loved me. But she died. A great love. And in Pretoria I went to the social workers' meetings and there was a Dutch girl there, very beautiful. But the preacher of the Gospel, he kept her away from me, he wanted her for himself . . . In America too there was a beautiful girl, an American, and in Germany one of the workers I liked . . . But I could not compete.

'My biological mother used to call me "Mimis". She liked me, but I was in love with her sister, Annie. The one with the wrestler . . . Can you remember Marlene Dietrich?'

I nodded.

'Aha!' he laughed. He began to sing, 'Falling in love again, what am I to do? Falling in lóóóve again.' The next half-hour went by with more songs ('Deep Purple', 'Jeepers Creepers', 'I Can't Give You Anything But Love, Baby') and a fond listing of the names of bygone film stars. Charlie Chaplin, Syd Chaplin, William Boyd, Douglas Fairbanks, Lana Turner. Buster Keaton remained his favourite, however, together with Dietrich. '*Bei mir bist du schön, bei mir bist du schön und wúúúnderbar . . .*'

Snatches of Greek, Italian and Portuguese songs followed. Of the Greek song he said, 'That one was very romantic.'

'Good morning.' It was one of the doctors, Dr Hamukoma by name, who had been drawn to the room by our singing. She tugged gently at the shoulder of Demitrios's shirt. 'How are you?'

'Adventures, adventures, all over the world,' Demitrios replied. 'Germany. The ships' bunkers on the river. Frankfurt am Main.'

Dr Hamukoma looked at me. She could not understand a word he was saying.

'Ships' bunkers. *Schiffsbunker*, with concrete walls, one metre sixty thick. I sat outside, to watch, in a little field. There were children playing. German children. They give me *Haselnüße*, hazel nuts, the small children. They pick them from the trees and give them to me. They were so kind . . . I didn't have any chocolate to pay them back.'

The doctor said to me: 'He's quite sweet.'

She was a slender black woman, of exceptionally attractive appearance. Why was it just then that Demitrios had to go right off his trolley?

'Now I want to give them something. I want to go back to the *Schiffsbunker*,' he said, starting to sob. 'I want to thank those children. They were very good to me, these girls, the small, little girls.'

And still sobbing: '"*Bei mir bist du schön und wunderbar.*"'

Dr Hamukoma comforted him, holding his arm in both her hands. I wanted to explain to her what he had been talking about, but it was impossible to give a context to his words, since she evidently knew little of his life story.

Demitrios: '"You laugh today, you cry tomorrow." Do you remember that song too?'

'He badly needs a hearing aid,' I said to the doctor. She answered that the money to get him one was simply not available. Recently they had unsuccessfully tried to raise funds to provide a similar aid for another patient. The money was just not to be had.

'I want to hear those records again,' Demitrios said, after the doctor had left us to go on with her rounds. 'I know the rhythm, I just have to pick it up. *Anything* you want to ask me, ask me. I will tell you. I have a very good memory.'

That was not exactly what I had come for. An interrogation. An investigation.

'I can remember everything,' he assured me.

I picked up pencil and paper and wrote, '*Eugenie Livanos.*'

'*Livanos*, 1942. I was working there in the bakery. Down in the machine room. A very big boat. A Greek ship. They had contraband on board. Narcotics. But I had nothing to do with it. The captain was all right. He taught me how to steer the ship. Took me on the bridge – port, starboard, 360 degrees. He protected me. But the crew – very rough. The engine-room crew tried to rape me. They tried to convince me to have sex with them, but I wouldn't. When we got to Canada the immigration authorities took me to the *Eugenie Livanos*. "Do you want to go back on this ship? Do you want to work on this ship again?" I was then in prison. I said, "No!" So they left without me.'

After a silence, and with the air of one passing on an item of information I might find useful, he added: 'A big percentage of homosexuals among the Greeks.'

'My father was very strict,' he went on. 'He always *watched* you, in case . . .' He made masturbatory gestures with his hand.

'He was an engineer. He sacrificed his life to a perpetual motion machine. And I continued in his footsteps. My brother was also a lathe-turner. But my biological mother, she spoiled my brother. In the morning she gives him eggs, fried eggs, scrambled eggs. He, not me. He was born with one leg first, out of my stepmother. Not with the head. She was screaming all night. It was a breech birth. That's why she is like that.'

His chin sank towards his chest and he stuck out his lower lip, as if sulking. Then he lifted his head, recalling something important.

'She made a big mistake in Lourenço Marques when a Portuguese chemist discovered that I had a tapeworm. He gave me some medicine, an extract, a powerful poison. He said, "You must bring the species' head. I must study it." I drink the extract and the following day it started coming out. I went to the toilet and half of it was out, two or three metres. But the chemist had said, "You must not throw it away. You must bring it to me. I want to study it." My stepmother said, "It's out, out." She put it in the toilet.'

He mimed the pulling of a toilet chain.

'A big mistake! A very big mistake! Two or three metres . . . I think it's still alive in the sewers, because it doesn't die, it's very strong. And the Portuguese chemist was very angry. He said, "Why do you throw it away?" But the sewer is still there. I want to study the sewer underneath the old house. I want to go back to the sewer.'

He gazed at me with amber-coloured eyes. 'You must help me.' And later, wistfully, after I had taken a photo of him, 'I want you to photograph me in front of my house, in front of my property. I want you to help me.'

When I got back to my room that afternoon I phoned Johannesburg. After following various false trails I learned that there was a social worker attached to the Greek Orthodox church who had shown some concern for Demitrios. In the evening I managed to reach her. She must have been more than fifty years old, but she had a surprisingly youthful voice. The ice was soon broken between us. She was pleasantly surprised to hear that she was not alone in still being troubled by Demitrios's fate. A wretched fate it was, in her view. Had I noticed how dirty he was? He should really have been moved into a private clinic. But no one was ready to put up the money to make that possible. The community – and there were eighty thousand Greeks in the Transvaal alone – was not interested in him. He was a man under a stigma still; people preferred to let sleeping dogs lie. In Pretoria there were also two half-sisters, stepsisters, but because of the political implications of his case the people in the community wanted to have nothing to do with him. Even at Easter nobody from the family went to visit him, though it was the most important festival of the Orthodox church. She couldn't understand it.

'And the authorities?' I asked.

Well, when Demitrios had almost died six months before, she

had received a telephone call from the Health Department. Someone high up, she assumed, must have given the signal for her to be contacted. She was told that in the event of his death the press should not be informed. No publicity whatever was to be given to the matter. He was to be buried quietly and only then would a brief press statement follow.

She had sat next to his bed for two days, accompanied by an Orthodox priest. He stubbornly refused to die.

She knew little of his background. He had never spoken to her about his past in South Africa. He was very uncommunicative when she visited him in the institution.

'Who are you?' he would ask her. And: 'Why do you come here?'

Still she did go to see him from time to time. He was such a dear, soft-natured man, and so lonely. What she could never bring herself to understand was this: that he had ever been able to commit a murder. Some day somebody would have to explain it.

The compassionate social worker was not the only one who found it difficult to imagine how deeply within himself a man like Demitrios would have felt the dilemma of the 'baster' – the bastard, the half-blood. How it must have maimed his sense of self-worth, and the hopelessness he had known as a result. Non-whites were generally regarded by the whites as dirty, animal-like, untrustworthy; but the half-breed was the worst, precisely because he was so close to themselves.

'You like chocolate?' The question had been flung at me seven years previously by a crowd of young Coloureds on a suburban

Cape Town station, as I emerged from the train with a young Coloured woman. She took my arm and walked on resolutely. I did not dare to look back at those who were taunting me. The anger, the mixture of scorn and envy in their voices, the surprise and derision, were plain. What they were holding me responsible for was also evident. Welcome to the real world.

Now that overt racial prejudice is considered in much of the world to be virtually antique, or at least is vociferously repudiated, there is a danger that the history of all those of mixed race in South Africa will be suppressed, rendered incomprehensible. Inwardly we white north Europeans are choosing to forget the contours of our own craziness, the overwhelming ugliness of our fear of bastardy. Simple. The Coloured was defined by what he was *not*. Not white and not black. Even the 'native peoples' were regarded as preferable to the half-blood; they were at least 'pure'; to them fragmentary notions of the 'noble savage' could still cling. But the Coloureds were neither noble nor savage. Far from it. They were the evidence-become-flesh of white depravity and deceit, and hence every Coloured person could be seen as a wandering object of shame. The sacred borders between species had been transgressed – what could be more threatening? – and this was the result.

Throughout his life Demitrios had claimed that somewhere in southern Africa there was a woman waiting for him, the love of his youth. Even as a figment of his imagination, however, this ideal figure threatened to produce for him dark-skinned progeny, who would bring to light the concealed, hereditary stigma of his bad blood. He could cross the line, go over, 'play white', though always carrying within him the self-estrangement of his dark conscience.

Or, once his wanderings over Europe had miserably ended, he could take on the role of the shamed and vengeful Coloured. He would destroy the loud-voiced chief of the white tribe. With or without the help of the tapeworm inside him, he cut off the creature's head.

A few hours after the murder Verwoerd's wife was heard to comfort herself with the words, 'God does not make mistakes.'

But Demitrios had needed no command from heaven to do what he had done. His deed was the direct consequence of sublunary traumas. The tribal sentiments of the Afrikaner were derived in large measure from some of the sentiments that Tsafendas had harboured within himself: a longing to feel truly at home, a search for acknowledgement, a conviction that he had spent too long a time wandering the wilderness. The Afrikaner was ready to maintain his homeland through violence, the violence of the state if needs be. His preoccupation with racial purity and unsoiled blood was central to that aim.

Which of the two, then, was more truly crazy: Verwoerd or Tsafendas?

It was hardly possible to exaggerate the importance of what Demitrios had done, I reflected in my room in that Krugersdorp hotel. The attack on Verwoerd was a proclamation of the end of the doctrine of apartheid, of the idiotic dread of 'racial mixing'. It presaged the hesitant beginning of integration. Of a mixed-up living together – the very idea that had horrified so many generations of white South Africans. Of the birth of the 'rainbow nation' which, in a bout of overexcitement and child-like honesty, Demitrios had called for in 1964.

I had never been able to find any words for the feelings which had overwhelmed me on the afternoon of the attack, in September 1966. Retrospectively, it now seemed that the power of madness had at that moment shown itself to be equal to the madness of power. The murder was a melancholy manifestation of being, as if nature itself was finally striking the balance between them.

On Friday 27 March I paid my last visit to Demitrios. I took with me a small Greek stringed instrument, a *baglamá*, in hope of diverting him. This time Ward 12B was not prepared for my arrival. During my previous visit I had merely said that I might be returning, and no one had made any objection.

On this Friday hardly any of the staff were in attendance. The Strong Man led me to a hall where Demitrios sat dozing in the middle of a group of patients. The attendant left us, locking the door behind him. I found myself in a long, narrow space, an enclosed stoep with a wall of rough brick at one end and rusty-framed metal windows at the other. Among the twenty-odd patients it was difficult at first for me to pick out the nurse. She sat bent over a magazine and made no acknowledgement of my arrival. Her sphere of action appeared to be confined to the corner of the room next to the TV, which was switched on loudly and which burst out with a great clamour every now and again. The noise was deafening; the smell in the room fetid and penetrating.

Watched by the others I moved a chair next to Demitrios. The man to his left shouted something I could not understand though it was clearly addressed to me. He was a muscular chap in a striped dressing-gown. Almost everyone wore a similar striped-blue dressing-gown, though many simply had it slung over their shoulders or tied by the arms around the waist. Demitrios was wearing his dressing-gown back to front. It made him look absurd. Next to him sat a man apparently incapable of speech. While I waited I could do little more than look about me in a placatory manner. Conversation was impossible here.

Demitrios woke slowly. We waved to one another; then he made another gesture of complicity, a scraping movement of his thumb against his cheek, which I alone, having spent some time in Greece, could decipher. What a crazy lot.

He had no slippers on his feet. His right leg was stretched out in front of him. Around the big toe was a gauze bandage, through which some dried blood showed. The plaster holding the bandage in place was loose, and some of it had curled itself under his chair.

Facing us sat a young man. On his head was an open wound and a few tufts of hair.

'He's an epileptic,' Demitrios said, almost inaudibly, and made a small circular movement of his hand – another Greek gesture, indicating that he was in a bad way. The man sat with his chair tilted dangerously forward.

When the Strong Man with the keys returned, I asked him if Mr Tsafendas could be brought into a room next door. With an ill grace, he agreed. We had to lift Demitrios into a wheelchair. He was disconcertingly heavy. The person sitting closest to him had to be unceremoniously moved out of the way. I saw bits of food lying on the linoleum and a half-dried patch of damp. Then each of us took Demitrios by an armpit and, with difficulty, decanted him into his vehicle.

In the big room next to the kitchen he recovered his breath.

'Have you got any chocolate?'

Alas no.

He mumbled a few words about the chocolate in Middelburg. Once again I was struck by his English. An English that was hardly spoken any more, and to which he imparted a dragging intonation, a certain emphasis on particular syllables that could only have come from the Greek.

I showed him the *baglamá* and strummed a little tune on it.

'Very interesting instrument,' Demitrios said. 'Small in size. Delicate sound. I would have liked to have been able to play it myself. Or the piano accordion. The organ. Before that I was interested in the bugle. That was in Middelburg.'

Then, in a whisper, 'Play some more.'

The *baglamá* has a piercing but attractive sound; I was glad that he was able to hear it.

'Do you play the violin too? The saxophone? That's what I'd really like to do.'

The next question came out of the blue. He asked me who was the President of South Africa now.

On my little pad I wrote the name 'Mandela' and showed it to him.

'Nelson Mandela . . .? I would like to speak to him. He's a very strong man.'

When I made a few movements with my fists, like a boxer, Demitrios laughed out loud. From the hall behind us a harsh screaming suddenly broke out. If a stone could scream, it would make a noise like that. Then came the sounds of crashing crockery and another loud voice trying to restore order.

Demitrios had fallen silent. If I was ever to ask the question, this had to be the moment. 'Do you remember Verwoerd?' I scrawled on my pad with suddenly awkward fingers, and handed it to him.

'I didn't know Hendrik Verwoerd personally.' Demitrios sighed. He thought for a moment. 'I had never spoken to him before . . .'

The racket in the hall broke out briefly once more. I heard the footsteps of Demitrios's Strong Man and the unlocking of the door that led to the closed section of the ward.

Demitrios moved uneasily in his wheelchair.

'I do regret . . .,' he stammered. 'I *do* regret . . .,' he said again and yet again, for the third time. 'I *regret* . . .' He took the paper and pencil out of my hand.

When he returned the pad to me I saw that he had written four words in untidy block letters.

I REGRET WHAT HAPPENED.

He began to cry. I took both his shoulders in my hands and shouted as loudly as I could, 'Never mind. Other times. Not your fault.'

'A whole other time,' he sobbed. 'I am not that kind of person. It was something that happened. It was not in my nature. Besides, I was sick.'

His striped dressing-gown had fallen from his chest. Poor Mimis. In what followed he placed the blame on the doctors. It was their fault. They should have operated on him. Why hadn't they done it? He pointed to his stomach. Why hadn't they removed the creature in there? Either they could not or they would not do it.

'It will not die. I'm helpless against this Dragon-Tapeworm. I cannot do anything. But they won't investigate. Too difficult and very complicated. At night when I sleep I see orgies. All imagination. Visions.'

Then he told me that while he'd been working in parliament, he had heard from a woman member of the house that Verwoerd was not an upright human being. It was one of the things, he wanted me to know, that had set him thinking of what had to be done. 'She came to me – I found out later she was a member of the United Party – and she said, "Hendrik Verwoerd is a very immoral person." You see? When she told me that I went down . . . and that's how it started. *She* stirred me. She made me angry.'

Again he began to weep; then made an effort to compose himself. 'I went down to the shopping centre on the Herengracht and I bought a knife. I went inside and I said, "Give me a knife." The woman gave me a little knife. I said, "It's too small. Give me a bigger knife."'

When he had fallen silent I wrote a few more words on the pad.

'Like a real Cretan,' Demitrios read slowly. 'Yeh,' he said calmly. 'Nature, hereditary nature.

'It's nature,' he said again, with an air of finality. 'Human nature.'

When we said goodbye he pulled me closely to him, embracing me with one of his arms, and pressed, between sobs, a fatherly kiss on my cheek and forehead.

The Strong Man was waiting to see me off.

EPILOGUE

EARLY IN OCTOBER 1999, at the beginning of the South African spring, Demitrios fell ill and was transferred to a ward in which the inmates' physical ailments could be treated. He was suffering, not for the first time, from a bout of pneumonia; a condition aggravated by chronic heart disease. After a few days, on Thursday 7 October, the eighty-one-year-old patient finally succumbed.

That he had survived for so long attests in itself to his resilience and staying power. At four o'clock that afternoon the superintendent of the Krugersdorp hospital phoned the Orthodox church in Pretoria and spoke to the lady from the Greek welfare organisation whom I had contacted during my last visit. The family had to be informed and arrangements made. Everything, the welfare worker was given to understand, should be done with the utmost discretion. As little publicity as possible was to attend the occasion.

In fact the media had got wind of the event almost immediately. The news of Tsafendas's death was broadcast on national television within hours and was a leading item in the evening's news services. The first reports said that he would receive a pauper's burial, since he had no immediate family to meet the expenses involved.

Strictly speaking, this was inaccurate. Two of Demitrios's half-sisters had lately been living in Pretoria; at the time of his death they were reported to be in Greece. It was not clear whether they were merely visiting the country or were now residing there. Anyhow it made no difference. For decades the two aged ladies had had no truck whatever with their wayward brother.

By Friday the welfare worker – acting as spokeswoman for the Hellenic Orthodox Ladies' Association (HOLA) – had consulted with Archbishop Ionannis of Pretoria. Together they agreed that the Orthodox church would assume responsibility for the funeral service. In coming to this decision they took into account, among other things, the signs of piety Demitrios had displayed in his later years. HOLA would see to it that a coffin was ordered and would make arrangements for the service. It was scheduled for the following Monday at the Aghios Andreas (St Andrew's) church in Krugersdorp, which served the small but well-to-do Orthodox community on the east Rand. Its priest – Demitrios Vergitsis – was willing to take on the duty, whatever risks might be involved in so doing.

By that evening, acting probably under pressure of the publicity being given to the event, Archbishop Ionannis decided that the funeral should be brought forward to the very next day. The authorities insisted that a strong security presence be in place throughout.

Saturday morning 9 October, a bright spring day, saw a handful of mourners converging on St Andrew's church in Krugersdorp. They were outnumbered by members of the press corps, who were in turn outnumbered by plain-clothes and uniformed members of the South African Police, the latter accompanied by several large, nervous sniffer-dogs.

Among those who had come to pay their respects were Patrick and Louise O'Ryan, the couple Demitrios had stayed with in Lansdowne, Cape Town, in 1966, and who had remained in touch with him, official discouragement notwithstanding, through all his years in prison and asylum. They had flown in at a few hours' notice. Also present were Aron Mabe, a member of the Pan-Africanist Congress, and Gagi Mohane, a member of the African National Congress. They were there in their private capacity, however. To a journalist taking notes one of them said, 'We are burying a human being whom we believe to have been a hero.' Apart from the police, no official representatives from government or the opposition parties attended the service.

The two sisters (née Tsafandakis) had either been unable or unwilling to have flowers sent in their name. Shortly before the service began a large wreath of white lilies arrived – it was the only floral tribute received – and was carried into the church. It had been sent by Liza Key, who had befriended Demitrios while making a television documentary on his life. She had also made sure that a plaque would be placed on the coffin by one of the reporters, a friend of hers who worked for the Johannesburg *Sunday Independent*. It read: *Dimitri Tsafendas 1918–1999: Displaced Person, Sailor, Christian, Communist, Liberation Fighter, Political Prisoner, Hero: Remembered By His Friends*.

Disturbed perhaps by the arrival of the plaque, or by the wreath of odoriferous lilies, the police dogs went into a sudden paroxysm of barking and pulling at their leads. After some palaver the police had the little building cleared. While the priest, the congregation and the attendant reporters dallied on the pavement, the sniffer-dogs did what they were trained to do. Nothing was found. The incident would have amused Demitrios greatly, I suspect. No doubt a younger Tsafendas would also have been gratified by the words on the plaque: Liberation Fighter, Sailor, Hero . . . Perhaps only 'Professor of English' was missing.

Once the police had given the all clear, Father Vergitsis proceeded with the service. He spoke of 'pastures where there will be neither sorrow nor mourning. Nor will there be judgement.'

Soon after midday the group of mourners straggled along a pathway through the cemetery adjacent to the grounds of the Sterkfontein Hospital. The grave had been dug in a corner used for interring the poorest of the poor: vagrants and those without next of kin. Mrs O'Ryan wept quietly, her husband at her side. The last rituals were performed. With a symbolic gesture peculiar to the Orthodox church, the priest poured oil over the casket – a re-enacting of the anointment which welcomes a newcomer (whether infant or adult) to the faith. Then the coffin was lowered, the pit was filled in, the mourners went their separate ways.

Mimis's burial place has since remained unmarked. No tombstone has been erected above it. No sign identifies the spot. It has simply disappeared among the mounds, rubble and tangled grass in the immediate vicinity.

NOTES

The career of Tsafendas has not previously been the subject of a book. So a few words on my rendering of his history seem to be called for.

Virtually all the information about him that is presented here is drawn from primary sources. From this very fact a difficult problem arose, once I had set about the task of trying to reconstruct the course of his life. Anyone who goes through an archive is bound to find in it papers which seem to grow in significance, even as a painful, contradictory sense of their limitations becomes more and more apparent to the reader. I could have chosen to present Demitrios's life as the sources themselves invited: as a collection of shards. But the result would hardly have been readable, nor would it have done justice to his predicament. In some instances, therefore, I have taken my cue from considerations which arise in the restoration of archaeological excavations.

Not long ago it was the practice to present the fragments revealed by such digs in the most naturalistic manner possible. In times earlier still a contrary principle of 'originality' was followed: curators did their best to bring order into the remains of the past and to make their original form apparent to the onlooker, often by way of some neutrally coloured infilling. Speculative additions to the material, however, were precluded. In both cases the aim was to show something that no longer existed; in both cases a measure of artifice had to be used.

The amount of material that confronted me was overwhelming. In the State Archives in Pretoria alone, I came on twelve large cartons packed with documents gathered by the security police and the Department of Justice (some of which have since gone missing). They had been assembled to serve as evidence in the event of a full trial – which had never taken place. In the time and space available I struggled to arrange what I had come across in the style of 'neutral restoration' described above.

The events of Demitrios's life, the places he visited, the people he met and the conversations he had: these are either factually accurate or are inferred from other episodes and from my conversations with the man himself. Inferences of this kind are indicated in the text by a kind of deliberate hesitation (e.g. 'who, if anyone, might have been pulling the strings behind the scenes' – p. 78), or are presented unambiguously as a form of scene-painting (e.g. 'he was joyfully applauded and thrown on to the sandy beach' – p. 68).

All that said, it would clearly be false for me to claim that my impression of his selfhood and inner consciousness was based exclusively on facts that could be established retrospectively. His innermost life – that which he *felt* – had to be grasped intuitively. A transaction can be verified. A dilemma (his dilemma) is much harder to delineate. To do that I had to rely on instinct, an intuitive understanding of his personality and the things that affected him. Needless to say, the endeavour was made all the more compelling for me by our having struck up an acquaintance.

It was my conviction – one sustained over the last decade by meetings I have had and observations on journeys I have made – that by means of Demitrios's story I would be able to render something of the South African trauma. In that sense my book is a cautious attempt to achieve an *anamnesis* – a bringing back to memory of that which has been forgotten. No matter how immodest the effort may appear to be, I wanted to present in bold outline my perception of his (and the country's) turmoil during the tragic years of apartheid. To try to recall the prior history of someone's illness is not the same thing as giving a diagnosis of it.

*

A full apparatus of notes would imply that I was aiming for a quasi-scientific objectivity in writing the story. That was never my ambition. Nevertheless I trust that the reader will find the notes and references below illuminating.

pages 1–6 'On 11 February 1955 . . . with the knife in his right hand': this detailed dramatisation of Demitrios's stay in the

Hamburg hospital is drawn from no less detailed reports written irregularly in a journal describing the course of the patient's illness. The notes were subsequently copied by the General Hospital in Ochsenzoll; and, at his request, were sent to Dr I. Sakinofsky of Groote Schuur Hospital in Cape Town (see p. 113). Subsequently they were found by me in the State Archives in Pretoria in March 1998. The faded, brown suit in which I dress Demitrios on his discharge from hospital is derived from a line in the verse of the Alexandrian poet, K.P. Kavafis, a fellow townsman of his between 1919 and 1925.

page 7 'the journalist Gordon Winter': those who wish to know more of this man, an unscrupulous servant of the apartheid regime, and a former golfing partner of B.J. Vorster, the South African Prime Minister, can study the self-portrait which he presents in his book.

pages 9 ff. 'Hendrik Frensch Verwoerd . . .': it has not been my ambition to give a full account of his life; all I have done is to mention (possibly to caricatural effect) a few salient facts about him which Demitrios himself would have known. See further *Dr Hendrik Frensch Verwoerd* by G.D. Scholtz (Johannesburg, 1974), a hagiography of more than six hundred pages, and, among much else, H.O. Terblanche, 'Hollandse Afkoms van Verwoerd' (*Zuid-Afrika*, August 1998).

page 10 '"basters" – half-castes': the first time Demitrios was officially categorised in these terms was in a letter from the South African consul-general in Lourenço Marques to the headquarters of the South African Police in Marshall Square, Johannesburg, on

29 June 1937. 'The above-named is a half-caste . . . employed in Lourenço Marques Kiosk about a year ago, but dismissed owing to his communistic leanings.'

page 12 'Emigration was an experience I too had undergone': at the end of the Second World War a third of the population of the Netherlands was ready to consider emigration. Between 1946 and 1954, before my own family's departure, more than 200,000 Netherlanders actually emigrated. Of these about a tenth went directly to South Africa. The migrants were subsidised by a bonus of 5,000 guilders per emigrant – in effect a kind of bribe or 'relocation allowance' (*avant la lettre*). In 1955 a special committee was set up for the celebration abroad of the festival of St Nicholas's Day. Another Dutch habit – the use of bicycles – was soon abandoned in South Africa: this means of transport was confined in that country to 'kaffirs and servants', according to Du Plessis, *Nederlandse Emigrasie naar Suid-Afrika* (Pretoria, 1956).

page 14 'How many South Africans were chased out of their cities during those years?': the first large-scale displacement of population, that from Sophiatown in Johannesburg in February 1955, fell directly under Verwoerd's ministerial responsibility. Throughout the operation he was kept informed in his office by the police through 'express telegraph'. In these telexes the police told him that the black population left their homes in a joyful spirit: 'many of the Bantus in the street appear to be in picnic mood'.

page 34 '*Erotokritos*': *Poiema Erotikon Legomenon Erotokritos* (Vincenzo Kornarou, Venice, 1713) is the national epic of Crete, which Katerina would without any doubt have known. I have seldom met a Cretan who has been unable to recite passages in the swinging metre characteristic of the island (a rhyming decapenta-syllabic distichon, I believe).

page 48 'Guilliema Conte, who had set up a gym in the city': there still exists a touching photo of a thin, dreamy, youthful Demitrios, with a bewildered gaze, seated next to the formidably muscled brothers Conte, who are built like a pair of wardrobes. Demitrios's face is narrow, almost feminine; his expression, vulnerable.

page 50 Demitrios himself gave me this version of how he first heard who his mother was. The same applies to the story of his adventures with 'Cora'.

page 55 'he attempted to enlist in the Portuguese army': this is taken from a statement made by Demitrios to the South African Police, after the murder. I am doubtful of its veracity.

page 57 '"Out of control"': these are the only words I have put in Demitrios's mouth which I do not know him to have literally said or written. The picture of his illness given here – in large measure my own reconstruction – is derived both from his later statements and from my knowledge of people in my own circle who, like him, have suffered from intermittent periods of profound psychic distress.

page 59 'his name once again surfaces in the official South African files': a confusion of identities sometimes worked in Demitrios's favour. The officials apparently received no guidance on the transliteration of Greek names; furthermore, he had himself shortened his father's surname. By 1939 there were in existence a number of separate files which actually referred to the same man. The Department of Immigration and Asiatic Affairs had papers about him in File G. 8226; the Department of the Interior in Files B. 3700 and B. 7771.

pages 61–2 'the tapering silver leaf of a shrub . . . to the docks': information given to the writer by Demitrios, March 1998.

pages 63–4 'attached to a hospital in Boston': his condition was described by this institution as 'Psycho-neurosis – mixed type'. In all, he was admitted six times to hospitals on both sides of the Atlantic between 1943 and 1947. Among them were the Seamen's Convalescent Home in Oyster Bay; an American army hospital in Great Britain; and institutions in Charleston, South Carolina, Ellis Island Hospital in New York and North Grafton State Hospital in Massachusetts. The diagnoses made in these places were diverse in nature: 'schizophrenia'; 'subject to a psychosis – type not established'; 'constitutional psychopathy and pathologically emotional'. Two striking points emerge. First, he fell ill regularly but was as regularly declared healthy and discharged. (The 'revolving door policy', this is called nowadays: i.e. the patient is confined from time to time yet is usually considered well enough to be at large.) Secondly, and more importantly, he was never taken into care in southern Africa, which suggests that he was generally in a calmer state of mind when living there.

page 73 'The move did nothing to change his luck': around this time – some weeks after the uprising at Sharpeville – the first, unsuccessful attempt on Verwoerd's life was made. During an agricultural show in Johannesburg, a rich English-speaking farmer, David Pratt, succeeded in shooting the Prime Minister in the head, twice, with a small-calibre pistol (a .22, in fact, like the one Demitrios was to buy in Cape Town, some seven years later). Verwoerd survived the attack in miraculous fashion: the doctors discovered that the bullets had done not much more than clear out his sinuses. In London money was collected for a lawyer to defend Pratt in court, but he committed suicide in a psychiatric hospital in Bloemfontein before the trial could begin.

page 79 'J. van der Berg, the official responsible': according to report, van der Berg was extensively investigated and interrogated by the South African security police after the attack on Verwoerd. Subsequently he was discharged from the civil service. He ended up with his family in a down-at-heel district on the outskirts of Durban, a broken man.

page 81 'never regarded as a hero': in part no doubt because of the attitude of the African National Congress. Their official account of the incident is that the deed was committed by 'an obscure *white* messenger' (my italics). The words are those of Nelson Mandela. He follows them by saying, 'Political assassination is not something that I or the ANC have ever supported.' *Long Walk to Freedom* (London, 1994), p. 417.

For a further indication of the post-apartheid government's

attitude towards Tsafendas see my extended note below, attached to a quotation taken from p. 00.

page 87 'Hanno Probst': Probst recognised an enlarged passport photograph of Demitrios in *The Natal Mercury* fifteen months after their meeting. He made a deposition to the police in Nyoni in which he stated: 'I suspect him (Tsafendas) of having had an influence over the inhabitants of Mangete . . . The youth in the reserve became aggressive and obstreperous while he was there. Since the assassination of Dr Verwoerd order has been re-established and the young men in the area, fortunately, are well under control.'

page 108 'Manolis, the tall bosun': Manolis Mastromanolis – then thirty-seven years old, today almost seventy – currently lives in his birthplace, the island of Kossos. He refuses to speak of the events described here.

page 112 '"We'll get the lot of you!"' – see *In No Uncertain Terms: Memoirs* by Helen Suzman (London, 1993, p. 69.)

page 112 'Verwoerd's lifeless body': the report on the autopsy – which was carried out by Dr Theodor Gottfried Schwär, in the presence of Lt Col Buytendag of the S.A. Police – contains an extensive account of the wounds inflicted on Verwoerd. It states also that his brain weighed 1.430 kilograms.

pages 115–116 'The sexual part of it too – the Immorality Act . . .': this information was withheld from the public. The same applied to Demitrios's seditious remarks made earlier in Mozambique about the rainbow flag, which were duly noted down by the PIDE. The Portuguese divulged this information on condition of its being kept confidential. The Americans were also reticent in the matter. A coded report marked TOP SECRET was sent from the US embassy in South Africa to the State Department in Washington: 'The Department believes that handing over information at this stage could have undesirable consequences . . . since [the] file apparently reveals that Tsafendas is quarter Negro or African.'

page 129 *Evolution of the Species*: obviously *Origin of the Species* was intended. The mistake was Demitrios's.

page 135 'Why was he still confined in the wretched institution . . .?': Within a few days of my last meeting with Demitrios I wrote a letter to Archbishop Desmond Tutu, the then chairman of the Truth and Reconciliation Commission (TRC), asking for some form of amnesty and reparation to be granted to him. In the light of the Commission's remit this plea did not seem unreasonable, for Demitrios's motives at the time of the assassination had been political as well as personal in nature; he had identified strongly with the country's Coloured and black populations and felt himself to have been part of a wider movement of protest. My hope in making this representation was that he might be allowed to spend whatever days remained to him in the relative comfort of a private clinic. At the time of writing I was ignorant of the fact that several months previously a similar submission to the TRC had been made by Liza Key, the film-maker mentioned in the Epilogue above. She too had pleaded for a reconsideration of his case.

During the latter half of 1998 Demitrios was moved to a more comfortable section of the Sterkfontein Hospital. I do not know whether this was a consequence of the approaches made by Ms Key and myself. What is certain is that after a formal acknowledgement my letter was passed on to the Ministry of Health, which procrastinated for a full five months before replying to it. On the eve of the publication of my book in Dutch (*Een Mond Vol Glas*), I finally heard from the Minister herself, Dr Dlamini Zuma. In her letter Dr Zuma thanked me for the interest I had shown 'in Mr Tsafendas's health conditions' (*sic*) and assured me that she was confident that he was receiving the care and attention he needed. 'As his personal safety is also of concern,' the letter continued, 'we believe that his present environment is conducive.' (Conducive to what, I wondered?) She then went on to explain that 'a private facility could not offer the secure environment required as threats to his life are still a possibility'. And to forestall any further questions I was told flatly that 'the State does not pay for patients in private institutions'.

So there the matter remained. And there he remained, to the end.

page 144 'the dilemma of the "baster"': I am indebted here to insights brilliantly expressed by V.A. February in *Mind Your Colour: The 'Coloured' Stereotype in South African Literature* (London, 1981).

page 152 'the eighty-one-year-old patient finally succumbed': according to a reliable source Demitrios had insisted on making a will or testament of some sort several years previously. In it he is said to have stipulated that his body should undergo an autopsy, so that his 'worm' might be exposed to the eye of science at last. I have unable to find out whether or not his wishes in this matter were heeded.

I owe many thanks to the staff of the South African National Library and the Parliamentary Library, both in Cape Town, and of the National Archives in Pretoria, who served me tirelessly. A word of gratitude is due to the doctors and staff of the hospital in Sterkfontein and to the countless South Africans who assisted me over the years with advice, action and a listening ear, and who supported me with generous offers of hospitality. I can name only a few of them here: Ernest Lindenberg and Hazel Moolman, Peter and Barbara Knox-Shaw, Antjie Krog, Derick Eaves, Ampie Coetzee, Breyten Breytenbach.

For the guiding artistic concept by which I have worked, I owe special thanks to my dear, living muse, Nicole Müller, without whose insight, patience and sense of humour this book would never have appeared in print.